Truancy
and
School Absenteeism

Ken Reid

HODDER AND STOUGHTON
LONDON SYDNEY AUCKLAND TORONTO

British Library Cataloguing in Publication Data
Reid, Ken
    Truancy and school absenteeism.
    1. School attendance—Great Britain
    I. Title
    371.2'95'0941   LB3081

    ISBN 0 340 36471 8

First published 1985

Printed and bound in Great Britain for
Hodder and Stoughton Educational,
a division of Hodder and Stoughton Ltd,
Mill Road, Dunton Green, Sevenoaks, Kent,
by Page Bros (Norwich) Ltd

Set in 11/12 pt Linotron Plantin by
Rowland Phototypesetting Ltd, Bury St Edmunds, Suffolk

Contents

Acknowledgments   vi

Introduction   1

1   Setting the Scene   3

2   Background to Truancy and Absenteeism   11

3. Non-attendance and the Law   23

4   Reasons for Missing School   41

5   Social Aspects of Truancy and Absenteeism   52

6   Social and Psychological Aspects   57

7   Psychological Aspects of Truancy   68

8   Institutional Aspects of Non-attendance   80

9   Educational Facets   85

10 Inside the Schools   96

11 The Guidance of Truants   108

12 Towards Good Practice   119

13 Truancy and Adult Life   124

14 Conclusions and Prospective Outlook   131

Appendix 1   Legal Cases Cited in Text   137

Appendix 2   Recommended Further Reading   137

References and Bibliography   139

Index   153

Acknowledgments

I would like to thank several people for all their help during the preparation of this book. First and foremost, I would like to thank my wife, Pat, for all her help and encouragement, especially for looking after Rebecca and the twins, Nicholas and Joanna, even more than usual! Second, I owe a considerable debt of gratitude to 'Young David' (Professor David Pritchard) for all his empathy, advice and encouragement. Sir, you are not only a real gentleman but a model professional. One day, I really will be nearly a quarter as good as you! Third, I am grateful for the help and encouragement shown to me by several members of staff at the Department of Education, University College of Cardiff, especially Nan Davies and Professors Taylor and Davie as well as Gerald Bernbaum, Professor of Education, University of Leicester School of Education. Fourth, I would like to thank Eugene Barter for typing the manuscript and Rebecca White for typing the draft chapters. Lastly, I am very much indebted to Diana Simons and Ann Simmonds – it has been a pleasure working with you. To you all, I am eternally grateful.

Introduction

This book is primarily intended to be of practical help to serving teachers and teachers-in-training. It is also meant to give valuable insights into the background, handling and treatment of truants and absentees for all those caring professionals (social workers, educational psychologists, education welfare officers and so on) who are likely to come into contact with these kinds of pupils. The purpose of the book is to show that truancy and school absenteeism are complex multi-dimensional problems, and that teachers and related professionals need to understand the issues involved in these phenomena if they are to stand any chance of successfully re-integrating non-attenders into their institutions.

The book is intended to replace and up-date Tyerman's (1968) influential study *Truancy* which proved such a successful starting-point for so many interested teachers and researchers. Unlike the earlier work, however, the book pays close attention to the ways in which teachers can manage truants and absentees by examining the educational implications of the findings in each chapter from Chapter 2 onwards.

Throughout the text, the book stresses the enlightened position which teachers need to take if the genesis and chronic stages of non-attendance are to be prevented or overcome. For example, it is contended that existing counselling and remedial measures used with truants and absentees rarely prove satisfactory. This is more serious than it may at first sound, because the long-term outlook for truants is not good and probably much worse than many people currently believe. The outlook for unskilled labour is very bleak. Therefore, the emphasis in the text is upon understanding, thereby removing difficulties, rather than upon mere containment or punitive measures. In this way, it is hoped that the text, case data and suggestions for practitioners will provoke teachers and other interested professionals into adopting more innovative and realistic positions which will help absentees and truants rather than merely punishing them for their actions.

The book attempts to show that most truants and absentees are not ogres. Rather, they are unfortunate human beings who are worthy of help in much the same way as the elderly, sick, or handicapped. All people are worth caring about – even those who may cause problems by their non-conformist behaviour.

And since truancy and absenteeism are multi-causal problems involving various combinations of home, social, psychological, institutional and educational factors, the book may be viewed as a multi-disciplinary text which has applicability to all fields of education and which is concerned with the teacher as much as the pupils.

The book has three basic aims:

1   to acquaint the reader with most of the latest research and other information which is currently available in the related areas of truancy and school absenteeism;
2   to discuss and synthesise the information whenever possible, and to place the findings in their educational context;
3   to promote good and better practice in schools.

Finally, it should be noted that this book is not concerned with the topic of school refusal except on those occasions where it is of considerable relevance in the ensuing discussion.

My Own Research

From time to time throughout the text, profiles of Persistent Absentees will be presented at convenient points in the hope of providing further illumination. These case data were mainly obtained from 128 Persistent Absentees and two control groups whom I studied and interviewed using social anthropological (Stubbs and Delamont, 1976) and text/question-naire approaches between 1977 and 1980 (Reid, 1981;1982a). The schools, teachers, pupils and social workers referred to in these extracts are protected by pseudonyms.

All the pupils came from the third, fourth and fifth years of two comprehensive schools which are located in a deprived and industrial part of a large centre of population in South Wales. The first control group was made up of pupils from the same forms as the Persistent Absentees (usually in 'B' or 'C' bands) and matched for age and sex. The second control group was comprised of academic ('A' band) pupils from the same years as the Absentees and also matched for age and sex. All the control group pupils were known to be consistently good attenders (see Chapter 10). Prior to each stage of the research, a pilot study was undertaken at a nearby comprehensive school.

I

Setting the Scene

Introduction

Truancy, mitching, skiving, dodging – call it what you like – is not a new phenomenon. The concept has been known for generations. It is now almost 150 years since Webster painted his well known picture of 'The Truant' which depicts two absconders standing outside their small school-room nervously peering in at the activities inside. In popular English literature, truancy is sometimes seen as a natural, impish act of escapism, which is likely to take place at some stage during the normal development of certain children. Why, then, should truancy be viewed as a problem?

There are probably five main kinds of reasons for this state of affairs: legal, educational, psychological, sociological and institutional. Legally, truancy is a problem because of the consequences for parents who break their statutory duties by failing to ensure their children receive a suitable education. Educationally, truancy is a source of concern because non-attenders generally tend to fall behind in their work which affects other pupils as well as themselves. Psychologically, truancy is symptomatic of deeper trouble within an individual and may foreshadow more serious conditions in both childhood and adult life. Sociologically, truancy is known to be linked with multiple adverse home conditions, low social class and deprivation. Institutionally, truancy suggests disaffection with school.

Many teachers have little sympathy with truants. As people primarily concerned with imparting knowledge, they tend to feel that good attendance is essential if pupils are to make satisfactory progress. Teachers are busy people. Their workloads and the organisation of schools ensure that very few of them have the time to know a great deal about individual pupils. There are even fewer opportunities for them to become familiar with and understand those pupils who have rejected schooling in favour of other apparently less educational activities. Some teachers are delighted at the prospect of instructing fewer pupils – especially those who can be troublesome, backward, or require extra attention in class.

These statements are not cynical, they are realistic. In some schools, even enlightened policies for dealing with truants have failed. Why?

There are several reasons for this situation. First, truancy is a multi-causal problem. Second, every truant is unique. Third, many teachers have little understanding of the topic. Fourth, there are few easy solu-

3

tions. Fifth, there is not a great deal of evidence in the literature of 'good practice' with truants.

Perhaps the best way to illustrate the scope of the problem is to look briefly at three cases before defining what is meant by the terms truancy and absenteeism.

John

Fifteen-year-old John and his mother live in a two-room flat on a busy main road leading to the docks in a large industrial city in South Wales. Jean, his unemployed mother, relies entirely on the social services and child benefit for her income and support. From time to time their flat is shared by a third party – a male guest who, if he stays for a while, is generally given the gratuitous title of 'stepfather'.

On most school days, John has great difficulty in killing time. Consequently, he remains in the flat engaged in monotonous activity ('I get bored very easily'). He endeavours to pass the day away by participating in such non-productive activities as lying in bed ('I sleep too much'), skinning mice ('It's not cruel – you've got to do something'), and throwing darts at an imaginary dart board drawn on a somewhat battered-looking wall ('I dread the landlord finding out').

The flat itself is barren and stark – no carpets, three piece suite, wallpaper, pictures, radio, television, record player, telephone or luxury items. The most substantial and useful pieces of equipment in the flat are two single beds, a long bench, a worn-out chair, kitchen utensils and crockery and an electric kettle. For several years before moving into the flat, John and his mother lived in an antiquated caravan which was located on the perimeter of a large council tip in a designated caravan park.

Very occasionally, John attends school, dressed in old, shabby, second-hand clothes, and yearning to leave at the first available opportunity. This is his way of avoiding further court appearances.

When interviewed, John claimed that school had lost its meaning a long time ago. He was not quite sure when this point had been reached, but it was certainly at the primary stage. Significantly, he mentioned that he had begun to skip school after he had first started to realise what it was like to be different from other children; in effect, to be poor ('How would you feel having the other kids stare at you all the time?').

John has two ambitions in life. The first is to find a job – any job ('I used to want to be a cook – now I don't care'). He has already experienced three forms of illegal employment, 'looking after a market stall', 'in a butcher's shop', and as a 'trainee chef'. On each occasion he was sacked when his real age was ascertained ('Why won't they let me work? We need the money and it gives me something to do').

His second ambition is to earn enough money to enable him to take his mother for a holiday. ('She's a lovely person but we've never been anywhere. Apart from when I was a baby we've spent all our lives in this dump. I'd love to go somewhere really nice. Someone once promised to take us away but we never went. He left soon afterwards.')

Martin

Fourteen-year-old Martin lives in a three-bedroomed council house on a notorious inner-city estate with his father, mother, three brothers and two sisters. In order to climb the stairs, they pull themselves up on a rope as the father used the wood to replenish the fire on a cold morning during the preceding winter.

Martin attends his local comprehensive school very irregularly. This causes the school no great concern as he can be a thorn in the flesh of even the most capable teacher. Martin's atrocious behaviour has resulted in his being sent home from school on numerous occasions.

Following his first suspension from school, a general practitioner was summoned urgently to treat him at home. A neighbour found him locked up and tied by a rope to a fixture in the outside toilet. She informed the police that he claimed to have been there for three days. Later, a confidential social worker's report confirmed the story. The social worker accused Martin's father of doing 'untold psychological damage which no amount of therapy would cure'. She predicted that Martin's conduct was likely to deteriorate rather than improve as a consequence of his horrendous experience.

Ann

Ann spends most days helping her mother look after her two younger sisters. None of the children attends school regularly. ('I don't mind what I do – shopping, cooking, washing up, or cleaning, so long as I stay at home.')

Ann's two favourite occupations are taking her younger sisters to the local park and visiting her grandmother. She can see no point in attending school as she believes that her mother needs her help and enjoys her company. Jim, her father, a long-distance lorry driver, cares little that his eldest daughter misses school. He believes that 'mitching' never did him any harm!

John, Martin and Ann are not atypical. Although some of their personal characteristics are unusual, John follows Tyerman's (1968) description of the average, isolate truant who comes from a deprived and unsupportive home background. He has a low self-concept and little ambition or drive. In layman's terms, he is a born loser. Martin is one of a minority of disaffected, disruptive truants whose life style at home and at school brings him into fairly continuous conflict with authority. Ann is an underachieving, parental-condoned absentee.

What is truancy?

Most people instinctively think they know what truancy means, but it is quite hard to define. On one occasion, when some undergraduate students were asked to try to define the meaning of the term, two of their better attempts were: 'persistent absence without adequate reason' and 'being away from school illegally with or without parental consent'.

These definitions were not only reasonable attempts but worthy of further discussion. Both definitions imply that truancy is a generic term which is used to cover any illegitimate form of absence from school. This is not the case. The second statement brings into play the key phrase 'with or without parental consent'.

Tyerman (1968, page 9) defined a truant as a child who is absent on his own initiative without his parents' permission. In common with most writers, he distinguished between truancy and other reasons for absence, such as 'illness', 'parental-condoned absence' ('with-holding', 'parental withdrawal'), and 'school phobia' ('refusal').

The Pack Committee (Scottish Education Department, 1977, paragraph 2.17) which investigated truancy and disruptive behaviour in Scotland, took the view that parental-condoned absence was in fact truancy. The members went on to formulate their own definition of truancy which was within the terms of their brief. This stated that: 'Truancy is unauthorised absence from school, for any period, as a result of premeditated or spontaneous action on the part of the pupil, parent or both.' It is interesting that this definition, created by a learned cross-section of professionals, relates so closely with the brave attempts of the two undergraduates.

Another recent approach to truancy is to avoid the term altogether. Eaton and Houghton (1974), Galloway (1976a;b) and Carroll (1977a, page 4) are three writers who prefer to use the title 'absenteeism' to 'truancy'. Carroll prefers the label 'absenteeism' to 'truancy' because it encompasses truancy and the superficially less serious forms of poor attendance at school. In addition, he believes the term 'absenteeism' does not carry with it the emotive connotations commonly associated with the term 'truancy'.

Carroll argues that the 'problem of absenteeism' is not just about non-attenders but is also related to the home, the school, the neighbourhood in which the home and school are situated and, in sociological terms, society as well. He hopes that his phraseology conveys with it the implication that there is much more to be considered than just pupil characteristics in the study of absenteeism from school.

Some researchers have avoided the term 'truant' for different reasons. I did so because I needed an operational definition which made sense of the way in which I selected my group of Persistent Absentees and their two Control Groups in order to make meaningful comparisons between them. Hence, I defined a member of my Absentee group as: 'Any pupil who, for whatever reason, was absent for a minimum of 40 per cent of the two terms immediately prior to the commencement of the study and contrary to Section 39 of the Education Act of 1944.'

This proved to be a safe definition as the overwhelming majority of Absentees were later found to have been away for *at least* 65 per cent of the year before the investigation began, many absconding from school since very early in their secondary careers. In fact, a fifth were found to have histories of non-attendance in their primary schools, according to their educational records. One can imagine what it was like trying to plan and maintain regular internal schedules with them, especially between December and March in the bad weather.

I was also conscious that my operational definition avoided the complication of explaining the precarious dichotomy between, for example, truancy and parental-condoned absence. Subsequent findings vindicated my decision because some of the Persistent Absentees could have been classified as truants and parental-condoned absentees on separate occasions.

Finally, one point cannot be stressed too carefully. In some circles, notably teachers and the lay public, the term 'truant' is used to designate anyone from the occasional absentee to the child who refuses to attend school. This is very dangerous. Hence, although this book is called *Truancy and School Absenteeism*, great care has been taken to use the proper terms appertaining to particular studies. From time to time in the text, however, the terms truancy and absenteeism are used synonymously where the context is clear.

Rationale

I have written this book for several reasons. First, I hope to change the way in which many people think about truancy and truants. I would also like to alter the treatment which truants traditionally receive from a correctional and punishment-orientated model to an empathetic and remedial one. Punishing truants for their non-attendance when they return to school generally only serves to reinforce the original deviant conduct and strengthen their institutional alienation.

Second, I intend to write a text which is up to date and synthesises our current knowledge. This is not as easy as it sounds because there has been an imbalance in previous work and there are few agreed criteria about how to re-integrate truants into an educational process which they have repeatedly rejected.

Third, I would like to dispel certain myths. For instance, a pupil's home background and social circumstances are not the only reasons why many children play truant.

Fourth, I hope to put forward some new ideas and develop existing ones. I am acutely conscious that I am doing this at a time when the

7

teaching profession is under attack from many sides (Roy, 1983). Normally, I am sympathetic to the numerous professional problems which confront teachers. On this issue, however, I have to admit it is my firm belief that:

a   teachers and schools could do more to prevent truancy;
b   in some cases, teachers can be blamed as much as or more than parents;
c   the genesis for much absenteeism lies inside schools, but too many teachers seem unaware of this fact and have no idea of their part in the process;
d   there are substantial differences between schools and teachers in the way they treat truants and regard their absenteeism problem;
e   most truants and absentees blame their schools and their teachers rather than other people or any other factor for their own non-attendance.

Teaching is not the only profession which can be criticised in this respect. Educational psychologists have not achieved very much in overcoming mass absenteeism. Their success with particular truants is difficult to ascertain, especially as they usually only see the worst cases. Social workers do not appear to have the collective or individual answer, nor do the courts, education welfare officers, counsellors, or the police. In fact, most preventative and remedial work undertaken on truants is generally very poor. All of these points will be elaborated further later in the book.

Theoretical Basis

Most books have a theoretical basis and this is no exception. The arguments behind my ideas are comparatively simple to understand. It is my contention that a pupil's home background and social circumstances are not the only, nor indeed the main, reason why many children 'mitch' school. There is no doubt that a high proportion of truants/absentees come from working-class backgrounds, large families, and poor housing, and have known familial distress of one kind or another. Nevertheless, a majority of pupils in similar circumstances do not miss school. Thus, the social and home backgrounds of absentees are only one part of an extremely complex jigsaw.

Although parents are legally responsible when their children miss school, on some occasions the reasons for the absenteeism can be beyond their control. Obviously, if parents have good relationships with their children, then they should know when their offspring have a problem. The fact is, however, that many parents do not have such good relationships with their children and are ignorant of their anxieties and behaviour when at school. If pupils are unable to discuss their problems with their parents, we should be careful before criticising teachers too severely. Nevertheless, teachers and schools have to accept their share of responsibility for truancy. In my own research it was apparent that a high percentage of Absentees missed school for such reasons as:

a   boredom in lessons as a result of inactivity;
b   falling behind in school work and not being 'assisted' to catch up;
c   an unsuitable curriculum;
d   perceived bullying, extortion, or internal classroom strife;
e   alleged teacher–pupil conflicts;
f   inadequate pastoral care/counselling;
g   feelings that school was a less rewarding place for them than their more able peers; and
h   being unable to comply with school rules and regulations (especially relating to books, materials, games kit and school uniform).

It is worth stressing that every truant/absentee is unique. While many truants come from similar home and social backgrounds, their individual circumstances are very different from one another. Consequently, it may be comparatively easy to persuade one truant to return to school and almost impossible to succeed with another. Before any remedial processes can be successfully implemented with an individual truant, it is important to have a clear understanding of his or her problems.

In my experience, most truants are extremely sensitive people. They know this better than anyone else. Generally, they are not loud-mouthed and unpleasant pupils. Rather, truants tend to be shy, inward-looking people, many of whom are grateful for any interest and help which they receive from empathetic sources. Most truants know failure and like most humans yearn for success. Their opportunities for success, however, are limited as they come from low income families and usually do not have the intellectual capacity to succeed with academic tasks in school.

While the social backgrounds of truants are well known (Tyerman, 1968), much less has been discovered about some of the school processes involved in non-attendance. The central importance of the relationship between truancy and schooling is only now beginning to emerge. For example, research has shown that even in schools situated in comparatively homogeneous regions, there are substantial differences between pupils' attendance patterns (Reynolds *et al.*, 1976; Rutter *et al.*, 1979). This suggests that schools and teachers have an important part to play in combatting the truancy rates in their institutions.

But this is very far from the whole picture. In my own investigation, for example, I found a number of interesting and interrelated facts. First, pupils from the same forms as the Persistent Absentees, many of whom also came from low social class backgrounds, appeared to attend school regularly for compensatory social rather than educational reasons, and they had significantly more friends in school and in their forms than the Absentees. Yet these good attenders generally had lower opinions of their schools and teachers than some of the Absentees and academic Controls. While the Absentees perceived their teachers in a less favourable light than their parents, friends or neighbours, a majority felt no malice towards them. It may well be that these findings highlight the failings of present pastoral care systems in schools and the fact that many good attenders are not entirely happy with their lot in schools, especially pupils in the lower ability bands (see Hargreaves, 1967; 1982). Thus, it is highly desirable that much more school-based research is undertaken into truancy in order to clarify and uncover the educational processes involved in this complicated phenomenon.

For all these reasons, it is my assertion that most truants miss school for a combination of social, psychological and educational factors. There is no one single cause. The precise reasons for the truancy will vary in particular cases. Indeed, there may be a major difference between pupils' initial and later reasons for skipping school. I think that most truants first miss school for comparatively minor reasons. Later, the same pupils are likely to 'mitch' for an increasing number of reasons. Once a pupil plucks up the courage to miss school for the first time, he or she is likely to find a considerable number of retrospective reasons to justify this behaviour. I am equally convinced that when the original reason for the absence lies undetected, the chances of persuading pupils back to school on a regular basis after they have reached the persistent stage are very low. Morally, teachers should not just tamely accept the situation when pupils miss their lessons. They have a duty to enquire into their pupils' actions and needs. Ignoring the problem will not make it go away.

2
Background to Truancy and Absenteeism

Before anyone attempts to deal with truants, he or she ought to have a clear understanding of the background and scope of the issues involved. Without this insight, people are likely to make mistakes. This chapter attempts to provide the sort of information which teachers and other professionals need in order to put truancy into its proper context. It covers eight topics:

1   historical aspects;
2   the incidence of truancy;
3   sex and age differences;
4   the special problem of South Wales;
5   non-attendance in Northern Ireland;
6   United States;
7   future outlook;
8   implications for practitioners.

Historical Aspects

No definitive study on the history of truancy has ever been written. There are, however, a number of accounts which trace or give clues on the development of school attendance at a local and national level (Booth, 1896; Simpson, 1947; Rubinstein, 1969; Roxburgh, 1971; Roberts, 1972; Ball, 1973; Withrington, 1975; Humphries, 1981).

Humphries's history of working class education between 1899 and 1939 is a reminder of the repressive nature of schooling in those early days when education first became available for all children, irrespective of status or ability. The widespread resistance which the introduction of compulsory education in 1918 provoked in the shape of truancy, classroom unrest, refusal to learn and widespread school strikes make compulsive reading. Apart from anything else, it helps to put some of our recent problems into their proper perspective.

It is worth recalling that the move towards compulsory education in the late nineteenth and early part of the twentieth centuries was gradual. Radical changes were needed in the thinking and attitudes of Victorian and Edwardian society before the change from voluntary to compulsory schooling could take place. In the event, over some 50 years the English ruling classes gradually shifted their position from employing child labourers daily for long hours and under unfavourable working conditions, to educating the same children in schools.

Attendance at school for all children between the ages of five and the recognised school-leaving age has been partially compulsory since 1870, and entirely so since 1918. In some ways, the 1870 Education Act can be seen as a watershed. Unfortunately, however, too little care was taken in the drafting of the relevant legislation concerning compulsory school attendance in the 1870 Act. This, and the prevailing economic circumstances of the era, are now seen as two of the reasons why so many parents subsequently remained indifferent or antagonistic to the whole process of schooling. Added to these legislative and economic difficulties were the unattractiveness of the buildings, the curriculum, and the teaching methods. The curriculum, for example, did not cater for the increasing number of less able and disadvantaged pupils who suddenly found themselves with an opportunity to go to school. Sociologically, the distance of the schools away from the home, the lack of transport and of suitable roads, and the hostility on the part of the gentry towards education for the working classes also militated against satisfactory levels of school attendance.

These problems left their legacies. It took nearly 40 years for average attendance to reach over 80 per cent in London (Rubinstein, 1969), and this experience was paralleled in Scotland and in urban areas where the School Boards were powerful and well organised (Roxburgh, 1971; Withrington, 1975). In rural areas, however, attendance remained poorer than in urban areas long after 1870 (Patrick, 1972).

In 1870, the School Boards were given powers to fix the school-leaving age. These boards were the first to begin to recruit the forerunners of our modern education welfare officers (Curtis, 1967; Maclure, 1967). Since then, there has been a gradual change in society's attitude towards the realities of what is involved in accepting compulsory education for all school-aged children. Significantly, however, considerable resistance was met particularly in parts of South Wales prior to and after the introduction of compulsory education through the 1870 and 1918 Acts where the rates of absence were often so bad that local associations were formed to award prizes and incentives for good school attendance (Reynolds and Murgatroyd, 1977). This is particularly interesting, not only because of the higher and disproportionate levels of absenteeism in South Wales today, but because the mining valleys were amongst those where child exploitation was rife and the working and home conditions of the population were very poor.

By the beginning of the twentieth century, academics were already undertaking investigations into the 'causes' of truancy and running away from school as it was sometimes called. In 1897 and 1898, Kline wrote two influential papers which suggested that 'running away and truancy are forcible protests against the narrow and artificial methods of the school-room; a rebellion against suppressed activity and a denial of free outdoor life'.

Despite all the social and educational improvements which have been made in schools since 1870, and despite the introduction of compulsory education in 1918, the variation in attendance rates in this century have been slight. While the national average hovers around 90 per cent, local (Rutter *et al.*, 1979) and regional (Davie *et al.*, 1972) variations abound. For example, the average rate of attendance in London of 80 per cent for secondary school children is no greater than it was 70 years ago.

It would be quite wrong to think that the problem of truancy is confined solely to Britain. India, Japan and Spain are but three countries which have similar difficulties. Even emerging African states are not immune. As far as we can ascertain, however, truancy is not a major concern behind the Iron Curtain.

By contrast, truancy is a serious problem in the United States where it was already a major issue by the turn of the century. Amongst a far larger school population, Abbott and Breckinridge (1970) have estimated that there were some 9799 truants 'in' schools in the States by 1889–90. By 1911–12, this total had risen to 62855. There are undoubted similarities between the development of truancy in Britain and the United States and these aspects will be referred to at appropriate points in the book.

The Incidence of Truancy

Most researchers now agree that valid and reliable measures of attendance are very difficult to obtain and interpret. In particular, absence figures which are based on school registers are notoriously unreliable especially, for example, because they do not exclude children who leave school after having registered (Williams, 1974).

The methodological problems involved in compiling attendance figures have been discussed in a short report produced by the Inner London Education Authority's Research and Statistics Branch (1980). Taken at face value, attendance registers tend to mislead and obscure true attend-ance patterns. An 85 per cent attendance figure could mean that 85 per cent of the pupils attend school all the time, while 15 per cent never attend. Alternatively, it could mean that all pupils attend 85 per cent of the time.

Both national and local surveys on truancy/absenteeism have been known to report vastly different rates of pupil attendance possibly because of the bias or standpoints of the researchers. Like registers, national surveys can be misleading; it is well known that attendance rates vary considerably throughout England and Wales (Davie *et al.*, 1972).

During the early to mid-seventies, attempts were made to measure the rates of attendance in schools. These findings generally show overall attendance rates varying between 85 and 92 per cent. The different surveys measured attendance during a day (DES, 1975; ILEA, 1976; 1980; 1981), a week (Institute for the Study and Treatment of Delinquency, 1974; National Association of Chief Education Welfare Officers, 1975; Barnes, 1979), a term (Galloway, 1976a), and a school year (Baum, 1978; Billington, 1978; White and Peddie, 1978; ILEA, 1981). The information produced by these surveys is sometimes influenced by the individual circumstances which operate within the school when these data are collected. Let us take an example from the summer term. The casual weekly non-attendance of pupils who are ostensibly preparing for examinations creates a considerable problem of continuity for teachers, which can be concealed by gross percentage figures (Baum, 1978).

Researchers who have studied patterns of attendance generally agree that they show a marked reduction during the day, week, term and school year (Trigg, 1973; Baum, 1978; Billington, 1978; White and Peddie, 1978; ILEA, 1981). The spring term is generally considered to be the worst term for attendance, probably because of illness and inclement weather conditions (Sandon, 1961).

The one-day national survey of all secondary and middle schools in England and Wales (DES, 1975) reported that 9.9 per cent of all pupils were absent on the day. Of these, 22.7 per cent (2.2 per cent of all pupils) had no legitimate reason for absence. This figure has subsequently been quoted as a probable national truancy rate (Carroll, 1977a). Owing to the way in which this survey was conducted, these figures have been considered by some education officers to underestimate the problem (Terry, 1975). Indeed, the National Association of Chief Education Welfare Officers (NACEWO, 1975) carried out their own survey in October 1973 of all secondary school children in 16 local education authorities. Their findings showed that 24 per cent of the secondary pupils were absent. Of these, it was estimated that between 3.5 and seven per cent of the children were away from school without good cause. In the Pack Committee's survey, which involved a six-week study of secondary pupils in Scotland in 1976, 15 per cent were found to have been unaccountably absent on at least one occasion (Scottish Education Department, 1977).

Sex and Age Differences

Truancy and absentee rates vary by sex and age (Shepherd *et al.*, 1971; Mitchell and Shepherd, 1980). Research has shown that there are major differences between the age and sex breakdowns of absentees when compared with truants. For example, at both the secondary (NACEWO, 1975; Welsh Education Office, 1975) and junior school levels (Douglas and Ross, 1968; Fogelman and Richardson, 1974), girls have been found to be more frequently absent than boys, although in classes of infants the reverse is true (NACEWO, 1975).

While most studies agree that more girls than boys are absent from school, a higher proportion of boys than girls play truant; Tyerman (1968) found that nine times more boys than girls play truant. In another survey undertaken before the school-leaving age was raised to 16, 77 per cent of the truants were reported to be boys and more than two-thirds were boys over the age of 12. The peak age for truancy was then 14 (Shepherd *et al.*, 1971).

For two reasons caution is needed when interpreting these findings. First, results tend to vary according to researchers' definitions of truancy. Far more girls than boys are known to miss school with the consent of their parents, yet many researchers do not classify these cases as truancy. Second, in studies based on clinical samples of truants, boys predominate at all ages. It is possible that some of these sex differences are due to the way in which clinical samples are selected. Truants referred for specialist help or treatment usually represent the worst or most extreme cases of this kind, frequently truant/delinquents or disruptive truants (Reid, 1984c). It has been established for a long time that delinquent behaviour is more characteristic of boys than girls (West and Farrington, 1973, 1977; Hoghughi, 1978) and it is hardly surprising that boys are in the majority. However, in certain schools and classrooms some girls give staff as many, and sometimes worse, behavioural problems as boys. It can be forgotten that girls, like boys, increase their truancy with age. The Institute for the Study and Treatment of Delinquency (1974) study found that, at the junior school, the girls' truancy rate was 0.6 per cent, increasing to 7.7 per cent by the junior secondary stage. The same enquiry reported that the boys' truancy rate varied between 1.82 per cent in the primary school to 6.7 per cent by the junior secondary stage.

The Department of Education and Science/Welsh Office Survey (DES, 1975) reported that for unjustified absence there was only a slight difference between secondary girls and boys – 2.3 and 2.2 per cent of all pupils respectively. At the junior school level, however, when teacher ratings have been used, a greater proportion of boys than girls have been considered as, or suspected of, being truants (Mitchell and Shepherd, 1980).

Rates of absenteeism and truancy can vary according to who is asked about them and what questions are asked. Fogelman and Richardson (1974) and Fogelman, Tibbenham and Lambert (1980) have reported on the findings of the National Child Development Project, a longitudinal study of all children born in England, Scotland and Wales in one week in 1958, when the cohort was aged seven and 11. Of the 1.2 per cent identified by teachers as truants at age 11, only half had poor attendance rates at age seven. Three-quarters of the truants were boys.

The cohort was followed up to the age of 16 by means of records and reports from parents, teachers and the pupils themselves (Fogelman, 1976). At age 14, average attendance was 89.4 per cent falling to 87.5 per cent at 15. Fifty-two per cent of the pupils themselves reported that they had truanted at some time for one reason or another, although the length of absence remained unspecified. Parents' reports claimed that 88 per cent of their children never truanted, 10 per cent occasionally truanted, while three per cent said their children truanted at least once a week. Whilst parents' and particularly pupils' reports are of much value, they are subjective and should, therefore, be treated with caution. Teachers' reports, considered by Fogelman to be the most reliable assessment, stated that attendance was considerably lower in the last two years of compulsory schooling. Of those reported to truant at age 11, 60 per cent were described as truanting at some time during the year at age 16, compared with 20 per cent of the total sample. Thus, once a pupil starts truanting, the behaviour is likely to persist (Davie, 1972; White and Peddie, 1978).

Truancy and absenteeism rates not only vary by age and sex but also by school and school types. Gray *et al.* (1980) found that absenteeism increases from about ten per cent in primary and lower secondary age ranges to approximately 20 per cent in the last years of compulsory schooling. Their London statistics show primary school attendance rates to have remained fairly constant over a considerable period of time. In secondary schools in London, however, non-attendance rates have risen from between nine and ten per cent in 1966–7 to 14 per cent in 1978. This is an interesting finding and provides some evidence to support those protagonists who argue that comprehensive schools and the raising of the school-leaving age are two factors which have led to the increase (Boyson, 1974; Reynolds *et al.*, 1976). Nevertheless, evidence to support a national rise in school absenteeism since comprehensive schools were introduced is flimsy. Without further research it seems as likely that absenteeism rates may have decreased or remained static in other parts of Britain over a similar period. However, much would depend on the operational definitions used by researchers as school types have changed considerably over the last 15 years, in some areas more than once.

Galloway's (1980a) report on the findings of the Sheffield Education Department's surveys of 1973 and 1974 reveal that an increase in absenteeism is evident at the age of 12, with a peak in the final year of schooling. Taken together, truancy and school phobia were thought to account for less than 20 per cent of absences, the majority of non-attenders being away with the consent of their parents.

Rutter *et al.* (1979), in their study of twelve Inner London secondary schools, found that the average attendance of the fifth year pupils during two weeks in September and January varied between 12.8 and 17.3 out of a maximum of 20 attendances. The proportion of poor attendances per school ranged from 5.7 to 25.9 per cent. These findings clearly imply that schools themselves are one of a number of aspects which affect attendance (others include catchment area and home circumstances). This contention will be considered further in Chapter 8.

In summary, research findings to date tend to show a somewhat confused picture, because of the variations in attendance rates between schools, differences in the way findings were ascertained, and differences between geographical areas and the age and sex of pupils, as well as seasonal, termly and weekly variations. Nevertheless, certain facts are reinforced by widely-found evidence: persistent absenteeism does increase substantially in the later years of schooling; truancy is a progressive phenomenon, reaching a peak at 15 and 16. The first and third years of schooling are critical periods in the lives of some disaffected pupils and it seems that many children initially begin to play truant at some point during this time either because of difficulties adjusting to life in comprehensive schools or because of disillusionment with teachers, the curriculum, or a host of personal, social and/or psychological influences such as bullying, falling behind in class work or problems at home.

The Special Problem of South Wales

It is a fact that Wales, relative to other parts of Britain, has the greatest problem of school absenteeism (Carroll, 1977a).

In some parts, attendance rates in secondary schools have been found to be as low as 50 to 70 per cent daily according to a variety of *ad hoc* local surveys. Reports by HM Inspectorate following inspections in comprehensive schools in South Wales have repeatedly drawn attention to the exceptionally low levels of regular pupil attendance in some institutions. The published report for Willows High School in Cardiff is but one such example (HMI, 1982). Of course, individual levels of non-attendance in some secondary schools in England, Scotland and Northern Ireland may be just as bad.

Rates of absenteeism in South Wales form one part of a complex and escalating debate on the standards of education in Welsh schools (Reynolds, 1982; Brace, 1982; Reid and Jones, 1983). In Welsh secondary schools, the rate for both justified and unjustified absence is greater than in any of the comparable English regions including the North-West, North-East, Midlands and Greater London. Likewise, at the primary level, the problem is more acute in Wales than in England and Scotland. Some educationists in Wales believe that the statistics provided by the national surveys for Wales are too low and underestimate the problem. Watkin (1975) has suggested that the real rate of absenteeism in Dyfed is twice that uncovered by the DES survey of 1974 (DES, 1975).

Evidence from two longitudinal studies of children born in 1946 and 1958 have shown that the higher rates of absenteeism in Wales than in England have remained consistent over a considerable period of time (Douglas and Ross, 1965; Davie *et al.*, 1972; Fogelman and Richardson, 1974). At the age of eleven, for instance, almost twice as many pupils in Wales (14.6 per cent) as in the South-West of England (7.5 per cent) failed to make 85 per cent of possible attendances. The truancy rate in Wales is also higher than in England: 4.1 per cent compared with 2.1 per cent in England. Carroll (1977a) has outlined the reaction of the general public and educationists to the special problem of absenteeism in Wales. This has taken many forms – including the setting up of committees, projects and research studies commissioned by the Welsh Office, local authorities and the National Association of the Teachers of Wales (UCAC, 1975; West Glamorgan, 1980).

A number of small-scale, but important, collaborative exercises between the social services and education departments have been tried and implemented, especially in South Glamorgan, and police departments in several Welsh authorities have introduced truancy patrols in some of the main cities and towns in order to reduce related acts of criminal damage, theft and trespass. Despite these activities, there is no evidence that the amount of absenteeism from schools in Wales is decreasing.

Vaughan (1976) and Reynolds (1982) have put some of the blame for the high statistics in Wales on three factors:

1   the tendencies for teachers to be more concerned with the able pupils than the less able;
2   curriculum development in Wales is less progressive than in England;
3   the concentration of much existing research on socio-economic factors, and on the child's personality, ability and educational failure rather than on the relevant institutional aspects, such as poor teaching, unsatisfactory curricula and outdated or unjustifiable school rules.

Much more research is needed before the reasons for the disproportionate relationship between the amount of absenteeism from schools in Wales and England is explained. Likewise, the contribution of absenteeism to the 'standards' debate in Wales has not been satisfactorily answered (Reynolds, 1982). As things stand now, approaching the second half of the 1980s, many of the possible answers and explanations put forward by researchers are based on informed guesses rather than fact. For example, the substantial differences between the social and educational backgrounds, previous work experience and training of postgraduate teachers in Wales and England have not been fully appreciated (Reid *et al.*, 1980; Patrick, Bernbaum and Reid, 1982). There is no nationally agreed common core curriculum on initial teacher education courses. The evidence shows that only a minority of postgraduate trainees take specific courses on truancy and absenteeism. In 1979–80, approximately two-thirds of postgraduate student-teachers followed some kind of introductory course on pastoral care and counselling. Only 40 per cent covered the topic of special educational needs of children with handicaps. Approximately one in four never undertook a course on the teaching of children of below average ability. Of the postgraduate student-teachers who covered these topics, most found them to be superficial rather than detailed, presumably because of the well known time constraints on PGCE courses. Moreover, the same research project ascertained that there are substantial regional, age, sex, social class, educational background and previous work experience differences between the intake of students commencing initial postgraduate teacher training courses, differences which are exacerbated by the students' experiences within the institutions and on teaching practice (Reid *et al.*, 1981; Bernbaum *et al.*, 1985).

Many new teachers are simply not trained to detect and work with deviant or disaffected pupils. Given the imbalance in in-service training throughout Britain, it seems probable that a high proportion of teachers have never received any formal training in coping with certain kinds of potentially disruptive and/or disaffected behaviour in schools and within their own classrooms. As a consequence, many teachers find things out for themselves the hard way.

This latter statement is supported by Reid *et al.* (1981) who ascertained that fewer than one in three of the same cohort of postgraduate trainees considered they had spent 'a lot of time' on such vital topics as 'control and discipline in the classroom' and 'classroom management and organisation'. This was despite the fact that a clear majority believed that failure to maintain order in the classroom was the one item which could make or break them on teaching practice and in their subsequent school careers.

Non-attendance in Northern Ireland

Moore and Jardine (1983) have reported the findings of a survey of persistent absenteeism undertaken during the spring term of 1982 among children of compulsory school age in Northern Ireland. They found:

1 A total of 19 417 children were identified as being absent for 14 days or more during the 1982 survey period. This represented 6.1 per cent of the secondary aged population in Northern Ireland, lower than comparative data for England and Wales despite the long history of trouble in the Province.
2 By comparison with a similar survey undertaken in 1977, this figure represented a drop of 1.7 per cent which suggests that absenteeism in Northern Ireland is on the decline rather than the increase.
3 As well as the reduction in the number of absentees recorded in 1982 to the number recorded in 1977, there was a general reduction in the length of absences. Approximately 80 per cent of all absentees were absent for a period of 25 days or less and 20 per cent for a period greater than this, compared with 70 and 30 per cent respectively in 1977.

The United States

Absence from school is also a major and uneven problem in the United States (United States Office of Education, 1960; Children's Defense

Fund, 1977; Bayh, 1977; NIE, 1977; NSBA, 1977; Rubel, 1977; NEA, 1979). Just as in England and Wales, major differences have been found in the behaviour and attendance rates of pupils by sex, age and geographical area. In parts of the States, the problem is so bad that some schools in New York, Chicago and the rural South report average daily attendance rates of between 40 and 50 per cent. Moreover, surveys show that pupil to pupil violence and pupil-teacher violence in some large inner city schools is rife, as are school robberies, vandalism, extortion, insolence to staff, indiscipline and racial conflicts. The evidence indicates that a high proportion of parents, pupils and teachers fear for their safety daily both at school and on their way to and from schools. The 14 to 16 age population appears to be particularly at risk. Reports suggest that there is a major breakdown in discipline in some schools. Even out of school hours, many teachers are attacked and their homes burgled or vandalised. All these factors have contributed to the high daily truancy rates amongst pupils and teachers alike.

Despite public concern about indiscipline in Britain, the situation in schools is much more under control, even in inner city areas and parts of the country where absenteeism, vandalism and delinquency rates are above average (Tattum, 1982). In some regions of South Wales, average daily attendance rates hover between 50 and 70 per cent and the related incidence of truancy and vandalism is high, but, generally speaking, teachers are in control of their classes and certainly do not live in fear of their pupils.

Future outlook

Two recent societal and educational changes could alter attendance patterns in the foreseeable future. First, it may be that the present lack of employment opportunities for lower ability sixteen-year-olds will lead to increased apathy and school absenteeism. Second, the initiatives implemented by the Manpower Services Commission through Technical and Vocational Educational Schemes and Youth Training Opportunities for 14- to 18-year-olds could seriously affect future patterns of attendance on British secondary schools. Further research will be needed to clarify these issues.

Present and future economic and social factors, as well as the impact of recent research, might also begin to affect parents' and teachers' attitudes towards truancy and other forms of non-attendance at school, especially as schools are starting to be made more accountable for their outcomes. How parents will react when they discover that their children are attending schools with poor attendance records remains to be seen. No doubt some will be more perturbed than others! It may be significant that absenteeism rates in France, where parents are made more accountable for the actions of their children, are much lower than in England and Wales. Non-attendance at school in France is punished by reduced child allowances for the parents, and in West Germany parents can be fined immediately when their children skip school.

At one time schools in England and Wales relied upon their attendance returns for the size of their grant and, not surprisingly, school personnel were particularly keen to enforce attendance regulations in order to protect their own salaries. Incorrigible truants tended to be severely punished and received separate treatment from their peers in an attempt to prevent their misdemeanours from recurring (Withrington, 1975). Just imagine the havoc that would be wreaked today if teachers' salaries were dependent upon the attendance (and progress) of their pupils!

Implications for Practitioners

The prevention of absenteeism and truancy begins in primary schools. Too many primary teachers ignore their duty in this respect. When a very young child gets away with non-attendance, there is little chance that later on he or she will worry about missing school at the secondary stage. I believe that it takes a great deal of courage for a pupil initially to decide to stay away from school. The action should be seen as a last resort – the withdrawal from school representing a plea for help. If empathetic assistance is not forthcoming, and the plea remains unheeded, the root cause of the problem will continue undetected and grow in intensity. This is not an ideal situation for either pupil or school as the withdrawal is symptomatic of the failure of both parties to communicate.

Primary teachers need to be able to distinguish between genuine absenteeism, such as that caused, for example, by illness, and deliberate non-attendance. Notes from parents need to be carefully scrutinised for accuracy. Many children of junior school age miss school with the consent of their parents in order simply to stay at home. Once this habit develops, it can quickly reach the persistent stage.

In my own study conducted between 1977 and 1980, I found that 18 per cent of the 128 Persistent Absentees began their histories of non-attendance in primary school. Nevertheless, only a small portion of these pupils received adverse comments on their attendance from their head-teachers before transferring to their secondary schools. This suggests that the information supplied by primary headteachers to secondary staff is not always as helpful or as accurate as it might be.

The transfer from primary to secondary school is in itself a traumatic experience for many eleven-year-olds, especially those who are known to be shy, come from unsupportive homes and experience adverse familial conditions. Some pupils soon feel lost as they wander, feeling very vulnerable, around the 'big' school, changing from class to class between lessons.

Another particular 'problem-time' comes at the age of 13 when most pupils decide which, if any, subjects to take in their public examinations. This is a sensitive time for many pupils. In my opinion, the non-examinee does not like to be labelled a failure; nor do some pupils like being forced to take CSE rather than 'O' level papers. Teachers need to use great skill to avoid 'creating' a rebellion on the part of some pupils which manifests itself in non-attendance.

The onset of adolescence and puberty at 13 or so is a sensitive time for many youngsters. Physical inferiority can lead to personality clashes with peers and teachers alike which also results in withdrawal. Demotions, promotions, class transfers, and the composition of sets need to be watched in this respect.

Secondary teachers need to be more vigilant in the winter months than the summer ones and at the end rather than the beginning of the day and week. Skilful timetabling of the lower ability forms could be a useful deterrent for absenteeism (Gillham, 1984). Spot checks should be carried out from time to time during the day in all schools. Registration periods do not detect specific lesson absence, early leaving or the vagaries of the smokers' union!

Good attendance should be the concern of all teachers, not just heads of year and deputies; in this respect, form and subject teachers are the first line of defence.

3

Non-attendance and the Law

It is vital that professionals – especially teachers – understand their legal position with regard to the non-attendance of pupils at school. The fact that many teachers, education welfare officers and social workers are dissatisfied with the way the law operates in non-attendance cases exemplifies the need for professionals to have understanding as well as insight into some of the legal complexities, especially if they are to take appropriate action in individual circumstances.

The Law

The laws on school attendance in England and Wales are largely covered by the Education Act of 1944 and the Children and Young Persons' Act of 1969 as amended by subsequent legislation, such as the raising of the school-leaving age and the Education Act of 1981. The local education authority can prosecute parents under Section 39 of the 1944 Education Act for failing to ensure their child's attendance at school, or under Section 37 for failure to comply with a school attendance order. On conviction, Section 40 of the Act permits magistrates to fine (or on third conviction, imprison) the parent. They may also, or instead, direct the local education authority to bring the child before the juvenile court under Section 1 of the Children and Young Persons' Act provided the child is under the age of 16.

Local education authorities can also bring separate proceedings under Section 1(2)e of the 1969 Act, which permits the juvenile court to make a care or supervision order on the child if '. . . he is of compulsory school age within the meaning of the 1944 Education Act and is not receiving efficient full-time education, suitable to his age, ability and aptitude . . . and if he is also in need of care and control which he is unlikely to receive unless the Court makes an order'. The local education authority has sole responsibility for initiating care proceedings in respect of school non-attendance, but will in practice liaise closely with the social services department, which has responsibility for initiating care proceedings on other grounds (Taylor and Saunders, 1976; Skinner *et al.*, 1983).

Scotland has a different legal system. Nevertheless, like England and

Wales, there is a similar provision for independent proceedings against parents and children. Section 35(1) of the Education (Scotland) Act of 1962 states that '. . . where a child of school age who has attended a public school on one or more occasions fails without reasonable excuse to attend regularly at the said school, then, unless the education authority have consented to the withdrawal of the child from school . . . his parents shall be guilty of an offence against this section'.

For the purposes of prosecution, a certificate produced by the head-teacher of the school is considered sufficient evidence of the child's record of attendance, which effectively throws the onus of establishing a reasonable excuse upon the parent. Whether or not the parent is convicted, the sheriff may refer the child to the Reporter of the Children's Panel with the expectation that this will result in an appearance before the Children's Hearing, which in practice has similar functions to the English juvenile Court.

The Education Authority can also independently refer the child to the Reporter under the 1968 Social Work (Scotland) Act. Section 32 of the Act states: 'A child may be in need of compulsory measures of care within the meaning of the Act [which can either be residential care or supervision in the community] if he has failed to attend school regularly without reasonable excuse.' The Reporter has independent powers of assessment and at this stage can decide that no further action is required, although the majority of cases are referred to the Hearing (HMSO, 1968; Strathclyde Regional Council, 1977).

Northern Ireland has broadly similar juvenile legislation to England and Wales. However, a review of legislation and services relating to children and young people carried out by the Black Committee (1979) has recommended a new juvenile court model with the separation of care and criminal proceedings. The Report suggests that voluntary supervision by an education welfare officer should be the first stage in cases of school non-attendance and if this proved unsuccessful a supervision order could be requested from the juvenile court under care proceedings, with the nominated supervisor usually being the education welfare officer. School attendance would not, of itself, be grounds for seeking a care order, although the breakdown of a supervision order would.

Thus, throughout the United Kingdom, school attendance is compulsory. Children who fail to attend school without a justifiable reason (see pages 26–7) are held to be breaking the law and both they and their parents may be taken to court. In England and Wales, the Education Welfare Service (sometimes known as the Education Social Work Service) normally has the responsibility for bringing proceedings before court for school non-attendance. In practice, education welfare officers are alerted by schools or by their own examinations of attendance registers to cases of persistent absenteeism. Usually, they will make visits to the home of the child in question to discuss the matter with the parent(s) in order to assess the home situation. Generally speaking, there follows a series of initiatives to try to encourage better or renewed attendance. In most regions, court proceedings are a final option when other measures fail. Occasionally, some schools have a policy whereby they encourage early court action to be taken against non-attenders in the hope that a short, sharp shock will work. Court proceedings are brought against either the parent or the child, although not normally both simultaneously. If the parents are the main target of the intervention, this measure may be preceded in certain circumstances by the serving of a school attendance order on them. In practice, if parents claim that they are not able to enforce the attendance of their child, the child is often prosecuted under care proceedings in the juvenile court. Thus, possible criteria for taking legal action are:

1. Section 40, 1944 Education Act: proceedings under this section are appropriate when: (a) the parent is thought to be guilty of an offence under Sections 37 or 39; *and* (b) the offence is caused by the parents' wilful decision or apathy; *and* (c) it is thought that the parent is capable of exerting proper care and control, *and* that the effect of a court conviction and consequent penalty will be to encourage him to do so more effectively.

2. Section 1 proceedings under the 1969 Children and Young Persons' Act are appropriate when: (a) the parent is thought to be guilty of an offence under Section 37 or 39 of the 1944 Education Act; *and* (b) the child is thought to be beyond the parents' care and control; *and* (c) *either* it is not thought that punishing the parent will enable him to regain sufficient care and control to ensure his child's resumed attendance at school; or it is not thought that punishment by the court will provide sufficient incentive to compel the parent to exercise the care and control of which he is nevertheless capable.

Interpretation of the Law

This section considers what is meant by parental responsibilities, compulsory school age, school attendance orders, acceptable excuses for non-attendance, the role of the school and teachers' duties.

a Parental Responsibilities

The attendance laws relating to schoolchildren and their parents are still primarily governed by the Education Act, 1944. Perhaps the two most relevant parts of the Act for parents and teachers to understand are Sections 36 and 39(2), the latter defining the words 'to attend'.

The Act states that it is a parent's duty to ensure that a child of compulsory age receives efficient, full-time education suitable to his or her age, ability and aptitude, either by attendance at school or otherwise. If a child of compulsory age who is a registered pupil of a school fails to attend regularly, the parent is guilty of an offence (Section 39).

Parents can be convicted for failure to ensure that their child attends school regularly, even if they have made reasonable efforts to ensure that the child leaves home to go to school. Hence, parental duties are not relieved by ignorance of a child's truancy, although this may be a mitigating factor in the final sentence (Crump v. Gilmore, 1970). The court need only have evidence of a child's failure to attend to convict (Dutchman-Smith, 1971).

Once a local education authority has been notified of the irregular attendance of a pupil, the duty of enforcing attendance passes to the authority, which may instigate proceedings against the parents or the child or both. The courts may impose a fine or a month's imprisonment, or both in the case of subsequent offences (Education Act, 1944, Section 40(1) as amended by the Criminal Law Act, 1977, Section 6). Court action and its effects are discussed in greater detail later in this chapter.

b Compulsory School Age

The Education Act, 1944 (Section 35), as amended by the 1972 Raising of the School-leaving Age Order, provides that a person who has attained the age of five years but has not reached the age of 16 is deemed to be of compulsory school age. Pupils may not necessarily leave school immediately they pass their sixteenth birthday as they are not considered for this purpose to have reached the upper age limit of compulsory education until the appropriate school-leaving date (Education Act, 1962, Section 9 as amended by the Education School Leaving Dates Act of 1976, Section 1) except under exceptional circumstances.

c School Attendance Orders

Once a child reaches the age of five, his or her parents must ensure that he or she attends school regularly. When a parent is apparently failing to ensure this, the local education authority may require him to show that he is, in fact, fulfilling that duty. The notice served by the authority must specify the time within which the parent must reply, and this must not be less than 14 days (Education Act, 1944, Section 37). Failure to comply with the requirements of a school attendance order is an offence. Penalties are as for non-attendance.

This legislation has been complicated by the Education Act, 1981. One of the provisions of the Act allows parents to have the right to select the schools which their children attend, provided a number of conditions are fulfilled. For example, there must be a vacancy on the roll of the nominated school, otherwise local authorities have the right to veto the request.

d Acceptable Excuses

The 1944 Education Act, and the wording of the Act in particular, has been responsible for a number of notable legal cases. For instance, the difficulties involved in defining the word 'full-time' has resulted in several cases being fought in the courts (Baker, 1964; West, 1965; Taylor and Saunders, 1976; Partington, 1984).

There are four acceptable excuses for a child's non-attendance at school:

1 An unavoidable cause, such as sickness (Edwards, 1955), but the word 'unavoidable' must refer to the child and not to the parents (Jenkins v. Howells, 1949). For example, to keep a child at home in order that he or she may look after a younger child, or children, does not constitute an unavoidable cause (Neave v. Hills, 1919).
2 Absence on a day exclusively set apart for religious observance by the persuasion to which the parents belong – Ascension Day (Church of England and Roman Catholics), Day of Atonement (Jews). It is not necessary for the children to attend a church service on the day.
3 Absence for which permission has been given by a person authorised to do so by the managers, governors or proprietor of the school. For example, a child can be granted leave of absence to take his or her annual holidays with his or her parents, provided the duration is no longer than two weeks and the holiday cannot be taken at another time (Schools Regulations, 1959, No. 12).
4 When the school at which the child is registered is not within 'walking distance' of the child's home and suitable arrangements for his or her transportation have been made by the local education authority (Surrey County Council v. Ministry of Education, 1953). 'Walking distance' is taken to mean three miles or under by the shortest possible route (or two miles if the child is under eight), whether a road or a cart track (Hares v. Curtin, 1913). 'Distance, not safety' is the test for ascertaining the nearest route (Shaxted v. Ward, 1954).

A local authority in Wales which temporarily suspended the provision of school transport for some of its pupils in 1984 because of the need to make savings in its education budget, found that one consequence of the action was to dramatically increase rates of absenteeism in some of its schools causing teachers and parents alike to petition elected members to reintroduce the status quo, which they succeeded in doing (see also Surrey County Council v. Ministry of Education, 1953).

Finally, it should be noted that exclusion by a school is not necessarily a defence in non-attendance cases (Spiers v. Warrington Corporation, 1954) nor is running away from school to avoid the cane (Happe v. Lay, 1978).

e Role of the School

Persistent non-attendance over a thirty-day period empowers schools to remove offenders from their official rolls. Happily, most schools and local education authorities either deliberately overlook or fail to implement this option, probably in order to avoid the administrative chaos which would surely follow, especially in some parts of Britain.

Unfortunately, schools differ markedly in their policies towards non-attenders. Far too many are inconsistent in the way they go about referring pupils to the local education authorities for prosecution under the attendance regulations. I have never forgotten my initial surprise when, after obtaining special permission, I sat at the back of a juvenile court as an observer and listened to a number of cases. It soon became apparent that court outcomes were complicated by a wide range of factors which could include reports submitted by schools, social services and the school psychological services. For example, Case A, a bright child of 15, entered court after being prosecuted for missing 12 sessions (six days) from the local Catholic secondary school for the first time in her life. She was cautioned and her parents fined.

Case B, 14, then entered. She came from one of the local comprehensives located in a deprived neighbourhood. Within moments of entering court, she was hurling abuse at everyone present. This pupil had a long history of truancy and disruption and made no attempt to hide her uncooperative attitude towards the authority of the court. Astonishingly, after listening to all the evidence, the magistrate adjourned the case causing the education welfare officer to leave the court shaking his head in disbelief because no immediate action had been taken. This case exemplifies the limitations of court actions which can be taken by juvenile courts in extreme circumstances. Both the education welfare officer and the school had been hoping for a more positive outcome to the hearing to ease their own problems. The following day, the deputy head of Case B's school told me it was a waste of time taking truants to court because all it did was to lower staff morale and encourage the education welfare officer to believe that his job was untenable.

Later in this chapter (page 31ff.), attention is drawn to the fact that the laws relating to truancy tend to operate haphazardly and/or differently in various regions. For instance, while the policy of repeated adjournment is popular in Leeds (Berg *et al.*, 1977, 1978a), it was not used in juvenile courts in Sheffield between 1976 and 1978 (Galloway, Ball and Seyd, 1981a).

f Form Registers

There is a legal onus on all teachers to mark classroom registers properly. All entries in attendance registers must be original and written in ink. Any alterations should be made in such a way as to make the original entry and the correction clearly distinguishable.

There must be an attendance register for each class, form or group containing every name in that class, form or group. The register must be marked at the beginning of each morning and afternoon session at which secular instruction is given. Any pupil who is out of class for a medical or dental inspection or treatment (unless hospitalised or receiving treatment at home) must be marked present (Administrative Memorandum No. 531, 10 May, 1956).

Periodic returns, giving the cause of absence if known, must be made on all day-pupils who fail to attend school regularly or who have been absent continuously for two weeks unless a medical certificate has been received. Apart from the statutory requirements, the methods of marking attendance registers are left to the discretion of the local education authority and delegated by the authority for action. It goes without saying that these instructions should be carefully followed.

Attendance registers are documents which may be required in a court of law and they can provide vital evidence in prosecutions for non-attendance at school. They are open to inspection by HM Inspectorate and by other authorised personnel and they must be preserved for three years from the date on which they were last used (Pupils Registration Regulations, 1956, 5 to 9).

The Children and Young Persons' Act, 1969

Before deciding whether or not to prosecute, the local education authority must consider whether it is appropriate, alternatively or additionally to bring the child before a juvenile court under Section 1 of the Children and Young Persons' Act of 1969. If the authority proceeds with the action against the parent and a conviction follows, the magistrate may direct the authority to bring the child before a juvenile court. If this happens, the authority must comply (Education Act, 1944, Section 40 (2) and (3)).

Hence, the Children and Young Persons' Act of 1969 has complicated the 1944 Act and means in practice that local authorities should consider whether, instead of or as well as prosecuting the parents, the child should be made to appear in a juvenile court. Moreover, the previous provisions by which proceedings could be instituted against a child for failure to attend school have been repealed (Children and Young Persons' Act, 1969, Schedule 6). Thus, failure to attend school can now constitute one part of the care proceedings in juvenile courts. The Act states that the court may make a care order if the child is not being educated *and* if he is in need of care and control (Section 1). 'Care' applies not only to the physical well-being of a child – his means and his comfort at home – but also to his proper education. Otherwise he is not being properly cared for (S. (A Minor) (Care order: Education) (1977), 75 Local Government Reports 787).

In some parts of Britain, certain local authorities such as Sheffield have provided themselves with a third alternative to formal procedures taken either in magistrates' or juvenile courts through the introduction of Education Committee's School Attendance Section (SAS) or its equivalent. The Sheffield School Attendance Section consists of elected councillors and co-opted representatives of the teachers' associations. It is serviced by senior members of the education social work service. The proceedings are formal. At a session, an education social worker states his conclusions about the reasons for a child's absence from school. Members of the committee then interview the parent and child. Subsequently parents and child are asked to withdraw while members deliberate on their recommendation. Finally, parents and child return and are informed of the decision of the committee. Galloway *et al.* (1981a) report that recommendations from the School Attendance Section in Sheffield are not binding upon the Education Social Work service but a helpful preventative measure which can be used to reinforce casework with parents and their children. Further discussion on poor school attendance in Sheffield takes place later in the chapter.

Comments about the 1944 and 1969 Acts

The 1944 Education Act embodies a key principle. No parent or parents has or have the right to deprive their child or children of the advantages of full-time education provided by the State. Under special circumstances, suitable home tuition may be permitted but this practice is not widespread. Nevertheless, local education authorities sometimes evoke Section 56 of the 1944 Education Act as a first stage in weaning school refusers back to school.

Section 56 states: 'If a local education authority is satisfied that by reason of any extraordinary circumstances a child or young person is unable to attend a suitable school for the purpose of receiving primary or secondary education, they shall have the power with the Secretary of State to make special arrangements for him to receive such education other than at school, being primary or secondary as the case may be, or, if the authority is satisfied that it is impracticable for him to receive full-time education, and the Secretary of State approves, education similar in other respects but less than full-time.'

The main feature of the Children and Young Persons' Act is that it aims to complete the merging of the provision for delinquent and non-delinquent children and the Act has led to closer links being established between school, the social services and education departments. In practice, however, the links between these institutions remain too tenuous for fruitful innovations to take place and this is an area where further research is needed (DHSS/Welsh Office, 1977).

The Children and Young Persons' Act has, in many ways, been a progressive step forward as it embodies a number of concepts which are different from those in previous Acts. These include:

1   the view that there is no single cause of delinquency; rather, delinquent actions are seen 'as a matter of chance, determined by local circumstances and social background';
2   the attempt to achieve early recognition and full assessment of the children's needs before the helping or remedial process begins;
3   the implementation of a variety of treatments for dealing with children in trouble according to each individual's particular circumstances.

Treatments range from supervision at home to short-term intermediate treatment and long-term residential care of different types.

The Act has led to truancy being considered as a symptom of distress which is seen as being allied to the social and educational problems of the individual child. However, this legislation has led to a substantial increase in the amount of work undertaken by the local social service departments at a time when their resources are scarce and inadequate. Moreover, as social work is organised on a generic rather than specialist principle (following the post-Seebohm Local Authority Social Services Act of 1970), there are few social workers who can be considered experts on truancy cases. As a result, truants, like families with handicapped children (Butler *et al.*, 1977; Wilkin, 1979), tend to be given a lower priority than 'crisis-orientated' cases.

Another difficulty with the Children and Young Persons' Act is that it has led to a conflict of interests between education welfare officers and local authority social workers. This is another issue which needs resolving.

Finally, therefore, it should again be stressed that children in Britain are not prosecuted for truancy under criminal proceedings as they are for other offences. Instead, as previously mentioned, parents are brought before magistrates in the magistrates' or juvenile courts whilst their children may also be brought before magistrates in the juvenile courts, if appropriate. Owing to the punitive consequences of such formal procedures, some enlightened authorities like Sheffield have introduced School Attendance Sections, or their equivalent, as another means of making parents and their children answerable for pupils' non-attendance at school.

Court Procedures

Court procedures provide another complicated subject for discussion. Magistrates' Courts have the following options open to them for dealing with parents in truancy cases: fine only; fine and direction that child be referred to juvenile court; conditional discharge and direction that child be referred to juvenile court; absolute discharge; absolute discharge and direction that child be referred to juvenile court; case adjourned *sine die*; case withdrawn; case dismissed. In practice, some cases are brought before the courts for a second or third hearing before a final decision is reached.

Juvenile courts have the following measures open to them for children's appearances: supervision order; supervision order following interim care order; supervision order with intermediate treatment; care order; care order following an interim care order; case adjourned *sine die*; repeated adjournments; case withdrawn or dismissed. As in cases with parents in magistrates' courts some pupils are brought back on more than one occasion before final decisions are reached.

According to the literature, adjournment is one of the most popular outcomes in truancy cases, the courts working on the supposition that a threat can be as effective as punishment. However, in practice, a threat often proves ineffective.

Berg *et al.* (1977) found that the procedure of repeated adjournments was the main method of dealing with truants in juvenile courts in Leeds. They reported that this method was more effective in getting truants back to school than supervision orders. By contrast, Galloway *et al.* (1981a) found that repeated adjournments were not used in Sheffield between 1976 and 1978, although roughly one in seven cases were adjourned *sine die*. Presumably these differences have something to do with local magistrates' policies.

Supervision orders are quite common in juvenile courts. In his London survey, Tennent (1970) found that about half the truants brought before a juvenile court were eventually made the subject of a supervision order. Supervision orders of one kind or another were made on more than half (51.2 per cent) the offenders in Galloway's Sheffield study. Conversely, in Leeds, Berg *et al.* (1977) ascertained that only a fifth of truants were placed on supervision orders and these children tended to come from broken homes. Retrospectively, they reported that parental support and their attitudes are crucial influences in determining whether policies followed by courts are successful.

Residential placements have been found to account for about 10 per cent (Tennent, 1970), 15 per cent (Berg *et al.*, 1977) and almost a quarter (23.6 per cent) (Galloway *et al.*, 1981a) of the outcomes of truancy cases.

Until 1971, a sizeable proportion of boys brought before the courts for truancy were sent to remand centres. In one study, Tennent (1971) reported that a third of boys brought to court for failure to attend school were sent to a remand centre. However, since 1 January 1971 courts are not empowered to send pupils to remand homes or approved schools but rather to community homes, or to assessment centres on interim care orders. Whether a remand home or approved school is substantially different from a community home is a complex, not just semantic, issue as the outcome tends to be the same (Berg, 1980). In the Leeds study, at least two thirds of those taken into care eventually went into a residential institution of one kind or another. Berg *et al.* found that approximately 40 per cent of youngsters not placed under a care or supervision order immediately were later sent to assessment centres on interim care orders which illustrates the difficulties courts have in making correct decisions first time even after allowing for professional advice and changes in children's personal circumstances.

Regrettably, being put into the care of the local authority can be a shattering and, in some ways, humiliating experience for the young person. Often too little thought is given to the fact that many truants have few of the home, social and intellectual advantages of life. As a result, to be placed and treated in the same institutions as some of their more disruptive and aggressive peers is hardly conducive to encouraging them to reform. Rather, being put into care can be the breeding ground of resentment and crime – sometimes understandably so.

This is not the fault of the social services who have too few options available but it is a matter of such gravity that new and more imaginative solutions are needed. Given the funds, and goodwill, such experimentation should not be beyond the bounds of possibility.

It is also noteworthy that a high proportion of young offenders first participate in criminal activities while they are truanting from school. Once again, there is much public disquiet about the fact that young offenders tend to mix only with their own kind which often compounds rather than reforms their criminality. Indeed, many young offenders serve more than one term on remand or in Borstal which suggests that favourable outcomes are very difficult to achieve.

The evaluation of court procedures in truancy cases has been the subject of two revealing projects. As previously mentioned, Berg, Consterdine, Hullin, McGuire and Tyrer (1978) compared the effects of two different court procedures – adjournment and supervision in juvenile court cases. These findings showed the superiority of adjournment over supervision in the management of truancy by juvenile courts.

The authors suggest three reasons to explain their findings. First, the effect on the family of repeated court appearances; not least the inconvenience. Second, the continued interest and involvement of education welfare officers in adjournment cases. Third, the experience and effects upon the truants of having to sustain repeated court appearances rather than the alternative of having occasional chats with sympathetic social workers. Berg (1980) considers that education welfare officers are much more concerned with the limited problem of getting a child back to school than local authority social workers or probation officers who see themselves as having a much wider role.

In a related enquiry, Berg, Butler, Hullin, Smith and Tyrer (1978) carried out a separate investigation into truancy and juvenile court appearances, using 84 of the 96 children on whom the two court procedures mentioned above were used. They found that three independent factors are involved in most truancy cases. These are anti-social and educational problems; adverse social aspects allied to parental complicity; and social isolation. It seems, therefore, that there is a need to distinguish between these three aspects when assessing the reasons why some pupils miss school.

Galloway *et al.* (1981a) report that the final outcome of parents' appearances in magistrates' courts in Sheffield over two years between 1976 and 1978 for their children's truancy (N = 157) were: fine only (41.4 per cent); fine and direction that child be referred to juvenile court (36.9 per cent); conditional discharge and direction that child be referred to juvenile court (6.4 per cent); absolute discharge only (0.6 per cent); absolute discharge and direction that child be referred to juvenile court (13 per cent); all other outcomes including cases withdrawn, adjourned *sine die* and dismissed (5.7 per cent).*

Thus, the vast majority of parents who appeared in magistrates' courts in Sheffield for their children's truancy were fined, either with or without a direction that the child be brought before the juvenile court. The rationale behind fining parents is fairly simple to understand. The imposition of a fine means that the magistrates find the case proved, and consider the parent capable of exercising adequate care and control over the child. The decision to impose a fine is presumably influenced by the usual considerations of punishment (for an offence committed), or reform (encouraging a change of heart), or deterrence. In fining a parent, magistrates are acknowledging that either a conditional or an absolute discharge would be inappropriate especially for parents who have already, in effect, received several kinds of warnings from the local education authority. The size of fine imposed upon a parent is usually greater for second or further offences than for first offences.

A fine and direction that the local education authority take care proceedings in the juvenile court may be regarded as an expression of concern about a parent's ability or willingness to exercise proper care and control over the child. While most parents and many truants probably regard referral to the juvenile court as an additional punishment, the magistrates see it differently. They consider it one way of safeguarding the interests of the particular child.

A conditional or absolute discharge reflects a less serious view of a parent's responsibility for a child's poor school attendance than a fine. Section 40 allows magistrates to direct the child to the juvenile court after acquitting the parent on the grounds that he or she was doing everything possible to secure the child's regular attendance at school. However, this option is only open to magistrates when a parent pleads not guilty. In practice, very few parents plead not guilty.

Galloway *et al.* found that the final outcomes of children's appearances before the juvenile court over two years between 1976 and 1978 (N = 126) were: supervision order (45.7 per cent); supervision order following interim care order (3.1 per cent); supervision order with intermediate treatment (2.4 per cent); care order (20.5 per cent); care order following interim care order (3.1 per cent); case adjourned *sine die* (14.2 per cent); case withdrawn or dismissed (11 per cent). Before a final decision was reached, 33 children were brought back twice, and two children were brought back three times.

*NOTE Eighteen cases were brought back for a second hearing before a final decision was reached; two cases were brought back for a third hearing before a final decision was reached.

Poor School Attendance in Sheffield

The branch of the Sheffield local education authority responsible for investigating and acting on cases of poor school attendance is the education social work service. In Sheffield, like many other areas, members of this service often decide to undertake casework with truants and/or their families, without resorting to formal action. In such circumstances, education social workers usually make home visits to ascertain reasons for a child's absence. These visits can result in a rapid return to school, or reveal complex family problems, or uncover communication or other difficulties between home and school. Education social workers in Sheffield then decide whether to act as an intermediary between home and school in negotiating a child's return; and/or offering the child or parents casework support with an early return to school as one of the objectives; and/or offering the family practical assistance in, for example, their application for a range of welfare entitlements, or assistance in solving problems which concern the child at school.

Consequently, in Sheffield education social workers have three formal options to them in truancy cases. These are requesting parents (and sometimes older children) to attend a meeting of the Education Committee's School Attendance Section, prosecuting parents in the magistrates' courts, or under Section 1 of the 1969 Children and Young Persons' Act, initiating care proceedings in the juvenile court.

Galloway, Ball and Seyd (1981a,b) investigated the outcome of the 472 cases in which the parents of non-attenders and older children appeared before the Sheffield School Attendance Section between 1976 and 1978. Almost two thirds of the parents (64.6 per cent) who appeared were given warnings and their cases kept under review. Fourteen per cent were prosecuted in the magistrates' court. The remaining parents were referred:

1 to the juvenile court (1.3 per cent);
2 to the chief education social worker to go directly to court without review if there is no improvement in attendance/behaviour (3.2 per cent);
3 to the next school attendance section meeting (5.3 per cent);
4 to the probation service or social services department (3.8 per cent).

In addition, a few children were referred for medical reports (1.5 per cent), or to a psychologist or psychiatrist (2.8 per cent). On a minority of occasions, the committee referred cases back to the education social worker for further investigation or casework (2.5 per cent). Finally, under special circumstances, the School Attendance Section Committee arrived at specific child-centred or parental solutions (1.5 per cent) which met the needs of the child and/or parent better than any of the aforementioned outcomes.* The Sheffield School Attendance Section Committee is a good

*NOTE The total of recommendations exceeds 100 per cent because of four dual recommendations.

example of the education welfare service extending the scope of its professional activity and responsibility since the publication of the Ralphs Report (1973). Increasingly, more education welfare officers are taking qualifications in social work, a situation which is not always appreciated by those teachers who regard education welfare officers as non-professionals.

It is interesting to note that, despite Sheffield's innovation, Galloway *et al.* conclude that, while in theory action taken against the parents or children in attendance cases should be relatively straightforward, in practice this is often far from the norm owing to time delays, the range and scope of the problems involved in each case, the large number of school absentees and the relatively few education welfare officers. These aspects are compounded by complications in the operation of the law in attendance cases, by professional rivalries and different orientations between the various disciplines involved and by the bureaucratic nature of the court machinery as well as the lack of professionals in certain specialist fields such as psychologists and psychiatrists. As a result, it continues to be true that school attendance all too rarely improves following court appearances irrespective of the procedures recommended by the courts. Sometimes, however, certain pupils improve their attendance immediately prior to a court appearance in the hope of influencing court decisions. It is as well to remember that court rulings are made in good faith by unqualified amateurs rather than by experts. Many teachers will know how difficult it is to agree on the pupils' final examination marks; imagine how much more difficult it can be to reach the right decision in a truancy case where there are few yardsticks and few instances of a successful outcome.

In passing, it is also worth noting that between 1976 and 1978 the Sheffield School Attendance Section Committee dealt with three times as many cases as individual magistrates' and juvenile courts (472 as opposed to 157 and 126 respectively). These figures may provide some support for the advantages of having a School Attendance Section Committee which sifts cases prior to further action, referring only the most serious to the courts as well as providing an alternative to court action in its own right. Thus, the formation of a School Attendance Section by local education authorities can be used as a kind of early warning to parents, as an advisory service and as the instigator of further appropriate professional casework, as well as providing an alternative to court action.

Prosecution Statistics

National statistics show that in 1980 there were around 4000 prosecutions of parents in England and Wales under the 1944 Education Act (Thomas, 1982). Also in 1980, 2230 children in England and Wales were brought before the juvenile court on care proceedings under Section 1(2)(e) of the 1969 Children and Young Persons' Act, on the grounds of non-attendance at school. This accounted for 1 per cent of all juvenile court cases, the vast majority of which were criminal prosecutions. Of the 4000 parents prosecuted under the Education Act, 3670 were found guilty, and of these 83 per cent were fined and 15 per cent received absolute or conditional discharges. Out of the 2230 juvenile court truancy cases in England and Wales, the magistrates made no orders in 15 per cent of the cases. Of the remaining 1900, around half received supervision orders and half care orders.

Local statistics indicate that prosecutions in 1976–7 involving both parents and children in Sheffield represented about 0.15 per cent of all pupils on school rolls (Galloway *et al.*, 1981a). Berg *et al.* found that the number of children brought before the juvenile court in Leeds during the school year 1972–3 accounted for approximately 0.014 per cent of the total school roll.

Statistics on formal action for truancy in Scotland show that in 1979 there were over 2500 cases referred to the Reporter on the grounds of truancy. These constituted 10 per cent of all referrals, for all grounds including offences. In a sample study, Martin *et al.* (1981) found that Reporters dealt with 15 per cent of the cases themselves and referred 85 per cent to the Children's Hearing. The latter were therefore dealing with about the same number of truancy cases as juvenile courts throughout England and Wales which cover a population ten times greater. The authors do not report what percentage of school rolls these cases represent, but it is clear that, for whatever reasons, the proportion is a great deal higher than in England and Wales. These differences are even more striking when it emerges that, because a lower proportion of offence cases were referred to the Hearing, truancy alone accounted for about one in six cases brought before the Hearing, compared to around one in 100 juvenile court cases in England and Wales. Once again, these statistics provide further evidence of the differential response to the phenomenon of non-attendance on the part of individual schools and local education authorities in different parts of Britain.

In Scotland, Martin *et al.* ascertained that the Children's Hearing discharged just under a quarter of the truancy cases, made supervision orders in 70 per cent of cases and orders requiring residential care for six per cent. When comparing Scotland to the rest of Britain on a measure such as the lower use of residential care as a court outcome for truancy, the differing proportion of truancy cases and their comparative rarity in the English juvenile court systems should be borne in mind.

Criticisms of Court Decisions

A view widely held by many educationists is that the actions taken by the courts in attendance cases are stereotyped and lacking in imagination. But what can they do? There is no magic panacea which enables the right or most innovative decision to be taken every time. Magistrates have to choose from a narrow range of options. Who knows, many of them may not like the system.

Court action appears to be more effective with some children and their parents than others. Again, how can magistrates, teachers, social workers or education welfare officers know this in advance?

Actions taken by the court are sometimes more effective in the early stages than later stages of truancy. Possibly too few schools are prepared to recommend that early offenders are taken to court on a trial basis. This is where the introduction of a School Attendance Section as in Sheffield can be so valuable. This reluctance is understandable for humane as well as practical reasons. If all truants were taken to court, the pressure on the courts would soon be unbearable and they would be unable to cope. Nevertheless, the view that a short, sharp shock will forestall later persistent absence has rarely been tested – certainly not in controlled experiments.

In one school I visited in 1984, I ascertained that only a small proportion of its regular absentees or truants had been prosecuted. According to the headteacher this was due to the attitude of the social services department, bureaucracy, the number of cases handled by the school's education welfare officer and by the local education authority, and to the natural reluctance amongst all professionals to prosecute in cases involving difficult home or social circumstances. Nevertheless, he expressed surprise upon hearing that fewer than five per cent of the school's persistent absentees' parents had ever been prosecuted for their offspring's truancy. In 1977, in two other schools in a different county, I found that this proportion rose to 28 and 31 per cent respectively for pupils aged 13 to 16.

Communication between the courts and the child guidance clinics, social services and other professional agencies is often considered to be poor (Gold, 1967; Home Office Research Unit, 1976). The Pack Committee (Scottish Education Department, 1977) considered that prosecutions for truancy in Scotland often have unsuccessful outcomes because they are invoked long after they can have any meaningful effect. Similarly, there is a tendency to prosecute disruptive truants, whereas those absent from school for social reasons are frequently dealt with by more sympathetic means.

Unfortunately, very little is known about the advantages and disadvantages of punishing truants. Similarly, not much is known about the outcome of social workers' interventions with truants and absentees prior to and after their appearances in court. Hence, little is known about good practice between social workers and their truant clients. Nor have the effects of the Probation Service upon truants ever been fully understood (Jarvis, 1966; Power *et al.*, 1972), especially as many teachers are ignorant about the work which probation officers undertake with young offenders.

Gold (1967) asked whether taking a child to court for truancy is either beneficial or necessary. His research showed that the actions of the courts contradicted professional advice in almost 30 per cent of the cases which he investigated. In fewer than half of the cases was there a 'favourable out-come' in the long run.

In the United States it is increasingly thought that the laws governing school attendance need to be changed to allow for more flexible and imaginative schemes to be introduced. Many experts believe that the legal process should be turned into a helpful and constructive remedial activity rather than being solely punitive. There is also concern in the States that legal jargon used in the courts in prosecutions for truancy tends to adversely label absentees as delinquent, rather than distinguishing between comparatively minor (missing school) and major (stealing, vandalism, assault) offences. Similar criticisms in England and Wales partially led to the introduction of the Children and Young Persons' Act in 1969.

Despite legislative changes in Britain, many experts believe that the issue of penalising truants has never been successfully resolved. Some of the more novel approaches which have been suggested in the literature for reforming truants include sending them on army manoeuvres for character training and asking truants to participate in special work experience or community schemes (Harris, 1974). As things stand, there is a clear link between a juvenile being punished in court for one offence and later graduating to a second more serious crime.

Implications for Practitioners

It is clear that the legal obligations involved in school attendance have affected the way in which problems of not going to school are dealt with by educational, medical and social agencies. Nowadays, most schools generally only take truants to court in non-medical cases and when the adverse social circumstances are unlikely to draw sympathetic support from social workers, which would counter a school's initiative.

The prosecution of black children can pose particular difficulties. For example, the offspring of Asian parents are often brought up to accept their traditional family commitments and responsibilities. The roles of both boys and girls in such families can be different from those of white children and occasionally when ethical beliefs and customs become confused with the regulations governing compulsory attendance at school tension results. In my own research, I found examples of Asian boys acting as substitute fathers (paying bills and so on) because their mothers were not allowed or could not make themselves understood. I also found that some Asian girls had opted to remain away from school because they could see no purpose in educating themselves to a high standard. In their culture, the female role is secondary and their place is in the home. I found this latter aspect to be a source of real bitterness to one intelligent girl who not only resented her lot in life but the prospect of an arranged marriage. Teachers and social workers should be aware of these ethnic factors in multiracial districts in Britain.

Schools need to formulate their own viable and consistent policies before taking pupils to court for non-attendance. Inconsistencies between and within schools only serve to further polarise and heighten the chances of injustice in what is, after all, a largely unscientific process.

Teachers need to understand and sympathise with the difficult work undertaken in their schools by the education social (welfare) officers, many of whom are untrained for their work. Too often these officials are not fully integrated with the staff with whom they operate and act on the periphery rather than on the inside. This practice is hardly likely to increase their effectiveness or encourage good school-education welfare officer communication.

Education welfare officers carry a great deal of responsibility although their actions can be undermined by decisions taken by teachers, social workers and the courts. This is what makes their's a soul-destroying job. Education welfare officers are often the first line of defence in that they can be the first persons to visit the homes in non-attendance cases. After making these visits and reporting back to the school, they have to decide whether return to school can be achieved by working with the child and/or family without recourse to formal procedures or, if not, what alternative actions to recommend and take. It is usually at this point that the education welfare officers' problems really begin as they can come into conflict with the wishes of the social services, schools and parents.

Finally, teachers should understand the *in loco parentis* concept as it relates to school attendance. The fact that a teacher does not know why a pupil is away is no excuse in law. The duty of a caring teacher is to know something about every pupil he or she teaches – even those absent from lessons. If teachers could show pupils they really cared about their attendance, then they might inadvertently forestall much potential absenteeism. There is nothing better than feeling wanted in life.

4
Reasons for Missing School

This chapter considers some of the reasons for pupils missing school and examines how recent research has added new dimensions to the topic, while pointing out that this work has failed to reduce or overcome the phenomenon. The chapter is sub-divided into eight convenient sections:

1   medical reasons;
2   persistent absenteeism in Sheffield;
3   the Northern Ireland survey;
4   the South Wales study;
5   feelings when away from school;
6   single or group absenteeism;
7   categories of persistent absence; and
8   implications for practitioners.

Medical Reasons

The vast majority of absentees are away from school for legitimate medical reasons, either illness or accident (Sandon, 1961; Mitchell, 1972; Tyerman, 1972; NACEWO, 1975). The National Association of Chief Education Welfare Officer's survey showed that the proportion of pupils away from school because of illness was greatest in the infant stage and least at the secondary stage; the work of Douglas and Ross (1965) and Fogelman and Richardson (1974) indicated that absence from school occurs less in the junior than in the infant school stage, possibly because most children have built up their resistance to germs and infections. All this makes good sense – ask most mothers about their children's induction into nursery or infant classes and the number of colds and infections which they subsequently developed.

The NACEWO (1975, page 14) survey showed that illness accounted for 69 per cent of the total number who were absent from school. Of the rest, the main reasons given were holidays (7 per cent), 'other causes' (7 per cent), family neglect (6 per cent), accidents (4 per cent), truancy (3 per cent) and school refusal (1 per cent). For reasons best known to themselves, the NACEWO felt unable to accept such a high figure for illness as they believed 'that a considerable proportion of the notes of excuse for absence . . . which the child takes to school are partially or wholly untrue, or betoken the over-protective parent'. On the basis of their own experience, therefore, they estimated that only about 40 per cent of the absences were for genuine medical reasons.

Sheila Mitchell's (1972) study of absenteeism in secondary schools tends to support the Association's contention. She found that only 50 and 56 per cent of the boys and girls respectively were away for genuine medical reasons.

By contrast, Reynolds and Murgatroyd (1974) obtained data from nine secondary schools over a single year which revealed that 75 per cent of pupils who missed school for any reason were away because of illness. Such variations between samples should not be considered surprising as any amount of local factors can come into play, not least epidemics and institutional and parental-related aspects.

The other problem with all this work is that statistics can be misleading. Probably some of the differences between these findings can be accounted for by the positions of the respondents to whom the questions were addressed: in the case of Mitchell's study, the teachers; in the NACEWO survey, the parents. For example, what is really significant about the NACEWO's results is that only 19 per cent of the absences were unjustified and illegal.

Of course, the medical absence category is itself capable of being broken down further. In such studies, colds and 'flu are usually ranked near the top of the lists. Children born prematurely have been linked with both lower intelligence than the 'normal' population and greater absenteeism from school (Weiner and Harper, 1966). Similarly, some absentees have been found to suffer from a number of psychosomatic ailments.

Of more relevance to teachers is the opinion of Stone and Taylor (1975) who have suggested that parents often keep their children away from school for longer than is necessary following infectious illnesses. No doubt, many teachers would wish to put the opposite view, feeling that some parents unwisely continue to send children to school when their offspring are clearly unwell.

Although illness rates are greatest in very young children, the work of Fogelman (1976) should serve as a reminder that a sizeable proportion of the school age population experience medical or maturational problems without teachers being fully aware of the psychological damage which can be inflicted on these youngsters. For instance, Fogelman's findings obtained from the National Child Development cohort study concluded that surprisingly high proportions of sixteen-year-old pupils experience a variety of medical-related problems including slow pubertal development, obesity, skin conditions, migraine, enuresis, asthma, convulsive disorders, clumsiness, visual acuity, squints, hearing and speech disorders. It is, of course, well known that many truants have marked physical and/or psychological features which deviate from the norm and tend to make them conspicuous. Popular examples of this syndrome are red hair, fatness, undersize, oversize, lankiness, clumsiness, over-sensitivity (especially pupils with an 'artistic' nature), fieriness, overt poverty (poor clothing), a dislike of compulsory activities such as games and swimming, handicaps of various kinds and unclean personal habits. Good as well as bad attenders may be sensitive to teasing and/or ridicule which results from their physical or psychological mannerisms. All teachers should be alert to these possibilities.

School refusal can justifiably be included within the medical category in official statistics because not going to school is the main symptom of the illness. This principle has long been accepted (Hersov, 1960a; Clyne, 1966; Kahn and Nursten, 1968). In some cases, illness may be one of the precipitating factors leading to school refusal. By contrast, truancy and absenteeism are generally regarded by most researchers as depicting socio-educational, rather than medical, problems (Tyerman, 1971). However, the possibility remains that some truants and absentees are more at risk than other children from a health point of view (Carroll, 1977a) due to their unfavourable home and social circumstances and poorer diet.

Persistent Absenteeism in Sheffield

The important Sheffield study undertaken by David Galloway (1976a,b) has been very helpful in shedding light on the incidence and nature of persistent absenteeism. In 1973 and 1974 the Sheffield Education Department carried out annual surveys which asked headteachers to provide details about all pupils missing more than 50 per cent of attendances in the course of a six-week period (1973) and a 14-week spell (1974). An officer from the Education Department's support service responsible for school attendance (the education welfare section) then stated whether or not more than half of each child's absences were due to illness. If not, the officer selected which of seven categories accounted for the greatest proportion of the absences. Cases where more than half were due to illness were excluded from the subsequent analysis of the data.

Galloway found that truancy accounted for little more than two per cent of persistent absenteeism in primary school children and 11 per cent amongst comprehensive pupils. Absence with parents' knowledge accounted for over 40 per cent of all absenteeism in both primary and secondary children.

Galloway's work shows that prevalent rates of persistent school absenteeism are remarkably consistent from the start of compulsory education until the age of 12. Thereafter, there is a rapid increase in absenteeism and truancy which reach a peak in the final year of compulsory education.

The Northern Ireland Survey

Data obtained from the Northern Ireland survey (Moore and Jardine, 1983) are equally interesting. The researchers found that 4.2, 6.1 and 14.9 per cent of the 5–10, 11–14 and 15–16 age groups respectively could be classified as absentees in 1982. There were few large age, sex or regional differences within these data except in the 15–16 age group. Physical illnesses accounted for most absences in the 5–10 and 11–14 categories but for only half of those absentees in the 15–16 cohort. Perhaps the most revealing statistics, however, are those for the breakdown of absence type for the non-medical cases. Of these, 68.4 per cent of the pupils missed school with the consent and knowledge of their parents (holiday, working on a farm or in a business of some kind, kept at home to look after younger children, other relatives or for some other reason, or they were absent for no apparent reason with their parents' knowledge).

Both Galloway's and Moore and Jardine's data confirm the findings of previous researchers which show that parental-condoned absenteeism accounts for far more unjustified absence from school than any other single or combined category.

The South Wales Study

I have (Reid, 1983b) presented evidence on the views of 128 Persistent Absentees at two large comprehensive schools in industrial South Wales on their initial and continued reasons for missing school. These findings clearly show that despite the Absentees' generally unfavourable home, social and educational backgrounds, a greater proportion of the pupils were inclined to blame their institutions rather than anything else for their behaviour.

Retrospectively, 28 per cent of the Absentees gave a social reason for first missing school (domestic, peer group influences, entertainment, employment). For instance, one third year girl stated that she first missed school to look after her cousin when he developed food poisoning. A third year boy claimed that he first 'mitched' school after he was dared to by a friend.

Sixteen per cent of the Absentees gave a psychological reason for first skipping school (illness, psychosomatic ailments, laziness). For example, one fourth year boy admitted becoming anxious after falling behind with his school work following an illness. Another fifth year girl said her absenteeism began in the primary school after she had endured a great deal of teasing and embarrassment because she suffered from regular and persistent nose bleeds.

A majority (56 per cent) of the Absentees stated that they first missed school for 'institutional' reasons (school transfers, bullying, curriculum and examinations, school rules and punishment, the teachers, a desire to leave school early). These included pupils who felt alienated from their schools ('I liked my other school. I hate the kids and teachers in this place and I wish my parents had never moved house'); those who disliked particular subjects, such as games, and those who disliked the institutional rules, staff or intra-pupil friction within school. These data suggest that parental and peer group influences, school transfers, and the curriculum are major factors which lead many non-attenders to miss school for the first time.

When the Absentees were asked why they continued to miss school, it was generally found that they had more than one reason for their behaviour. When the total number of responses was broken down into the three major categories, it was found that 40, 24 and 86 per cent of the pupils respectively gave a social, psychological and/or institutional reason for continuing to miss school on a regular basis. Significantly, there was a large increase in the number of pupils who claimed they were continuing to miss school because of alleged bullying, the curriculum and examinations, school rules and punishment, the teachers and because they wanted to leave school altogether.

One of the main reasons for the substantial difference between my work and previous studies may be that Absentees rather than parents or teachers were asked the questions. Clearly, not all pupils will always tell the truth but at least they ought to know why they miss school better than secondary sources – teachers, social workers and education welfare officers. Possibly the truth lies somewhere between the extremes.

Some of my findings are worthy of further discussion. Only three pupils started to miss school before the age of eight. Eighteen per cent of the Absentees, however, admitted having begun deliberately to miss school prior to their transfer to the secondary stage. Almost one third (32 per cent) began to miss school in the year following this transfer. Of these, only half of the pupils gave the transfer as their initial reason for their absenteeism. A very small minority of the pupils (5 per cent) – all girls – began their histories of absenteeism after the age of 14. A quarter of the Absentees began to miss school at some point during the third year of their secondary education. These findings suggest that the three critical periods for the onset of school absenteeism are the last two years of primary education, and the first and third years of secondary schooling. In the latter instance, the segregation of pupils into academic and non-academic groups appears to have a considerable effect. Undoubtedly, unsatisfactory subject groupings caused a lowering of morale amongst some of the Absentees.

The evidence indicated that slightly more boys than girls (up to the age of twelve) had early histories of non-attendance at school. A higher proportion of girls than boys gave domestic or curricular reasons for initially missing and continuing to miss school. These facts confirm some of Galloway's (1980a) findings. More boys than girls appeared to have been influenced by their peers and by what they described as acts of bullying and extortion.

45

There was a large increase in the number of reasons given by the Absentees for continuing to miss school compared with the reason for their first absence. This applied to each of the three major categories (social, psychological and institutional) but was most noticeable in the large number of additional educational reasons given for missing school. These data suggest that there is a natural tendency amongst absentees to blame their schools and their teachers rather than themselves or their homes for their continued non-attendance, possibly as a means of justifying and rationalising their own behaviour. There is a hidden danger that some schools might become the scapegoats for absenteeism when in reality the genesis may have a very different cause. This tendency is balanced by the fact that actions which take place within schools may produce the specific stimuli for the withdrawal, even though educationists and other professionals may not always be aware of the situation. Future work will need to take these possibilities into account if objectivity is to be maintained, especially as there is little doubt that local factors played their part in Reid's findings. The fact, for example, that bullying (18.8 per cent) was so frequently mentioned by the Absentees highlighted a major problem in one of the two schools. Much more research is needed before definitive categories of absenteeism can be delineated, particularly as it can always be argued that every case is unique and contains an element of social, psychological and institutional aspects.

A further worrying trend is highlighted in my work. The reasons given by the 24 non-white Absentees in the sample suggests that the traditional cultural influences exerted upon certain black male and female pupils means that the non-attendance of these pupils has a number of different origins from their white peers. Generally speaking, the non-white Absentees appeared to be more influenced by domestic, curriculum (especially disenchantment at the limited English and mathematics help available) and bullying factors than other pupils. Once again, further research is needed from a larger sample, before firm conclusions can be reached on this issue.

My work also suggests that parental-condoned absenteeism is often too broad a category which masks the real reasons for pupils missing school. While many pupils (especially girls) may claim that they are staying away from school in order to help their parents, the truth could be very different – such as a dislike of certain lessons.

Feelings when away from School

Irrespective of the reason for non-attendance, I found that missing school was a profoundly unsatisfactory experience for the vast majority of the Absentees. Only a minority stated that they were 'pleased' or 'did not care'. Indeed, a small proportion indicated to me that they wished circumstances could be found whereby they could start again in school

46

with a clean sheet. This poses an interesting psychological question. Why do so many absentees elect to miss school when their behaviour causes them considerable anxiety, worry, fear and guilt? Although this concern is self-imposed, there can be little doubt that the resultant worry is at least equal to any pressure exerted on the pupils by staff in schools. Seen in this light, the Absentees' plight is even more pitiful.

The following verbatim statements indicate the sort of mental pressure to which the Absentees felt subjected.

'I just know I've got to go back sometime to face them. The longer I carry on the worse I make it for myself' (fifth year boy).

'. . . I worry all the time in case a teacher or someone else sees me in town and I get caught' (fifth year girl).

'I feel guilty about coming back to school . . . you have to make up some stupid lies about why you've been away . . . I keep telling them I've had the 'flu. . . . They know it's not true. . . . This makes walking around the school worse. . . .' (fifth year boy).

A darkening picture of the Persistent Absentees' daily lives was obtained by enquiring into what they did when they were away from school and the findings suggest that boredom is a major problem. In a number of cases the data were almost pathetic, illustrating the desperate search for activities which while time away as satisfactorily as possible.

The activities referred to by the Absentees included doing domestic chores, watching television, going to 'Bingo', staying in bed, lazing around the house, looking after siblings, visiting relatives, wandering around streets, walking around the city centre, sitting by the river, playing with pets, fishing, 'hiding' in another school, catching rabbits in woods, smoking, helping travelling people with their horses, playing football, training, swimming, visiting cafes, listening to records, visiting girl-friends, playing cards, going to dancing classes, helping a building contractor and attending drama rehearsals. The activities were divided into broad categories: domestic, wandering and social. It is somewhat ironic that in this technological age the kinds of activities undertaken by school absentees have not changed much in over 100 years.

Single or Group Absenteeism

Although a majority of the Persistent Absentees (60 per cent) claimed to spend most of their time on their own when away from school, 17 per cent stated that they only participated in group absenteeism, while the remainder (23 per cent) alternated between single and group activities. Evidence was found of familial absenteeism as well as planned and on the spur of the moment absenteeism. Sometimes, pupils began their absenteeism alone and then graduated to group absenteeism as, for example, one group which met either in a local park or in a nearby cafe.

The size of the Absentee groups was found to vary between two and six with a mean of approximately three. These data indicate that more boys than girls absent themselves from schools in groups. Conversely, more girls than boys are likely to remain at home, visit friends or relatives' homes, shop or visit town. According to the pupils, more boys than girls indulge in 'delinquent' activities (see Chapter 6).

Parental Attitudes

According to the Absentees, 65 per cent of their parents disapproved of their non-attendance at school; nine per cent 'approved', while 26 per cent of the parents were considered ambivalent. Clearly, there is a great deal of difference between tacit parental approval and outright disapproval, although there was very little overt evidence of parents actively collaborating with the schools in getting their offspring back to school. However, there are undoubtedly major differences between the 'hardened' attitudes of parents of chronic truants and of parents of first offenders.

In over half the cases where parental disapproval was acknowledged, the Absentees stated that on occasion family quarrels and/or 'rifts' took place within the home because of their non-attendance. These quarrels were especially rife following threats of prosecution, letters from the school and home visits by educational welfare officers. Despite the majority disapproval, only 15 per cent of the parents took any form of 'positive' action against their children in order to discourage their non-attendance. Measures mentioned by the Absentees included the stopping of pocket money, returning them to the school gates and detaining them at home in the evenings. Many of the Absentees specifically mentioned that they disliked being punished by their parents far more than their schools and, according to the Absentees, it seems that a large proportion of the parents simply took the easy way out by '. . . just telling me to return to school and then doing nothing about it', or '. . . telling me off and then sending the school a false note'.

Categories of Persistent Absence

My work suggests that future researchers should endeavour to sub-divide large samples of absentees into more meaningful categories. To assume that all truants and absentees miss school for the same reasons is unhelpful and can be misleading. Unless such categories emerge, there will continue to be a danger of teachers, social workers and other interested professionals attributing similar tendencies to all non-attenders, irrespective of cause.

The four categories I have suggested are the Traditional (or Typical) Absentee, the Institutional Absentee, the Psychological Absentee, and the Generic Absentee. Much more research is needed before these classifications are tightened. It may be that considerable amendments will be needed for this to be achieved especially as the work was undertaken on only 128 Absentees from a deprived neighbourhood. The result of tightening these constructs would be to open up numerous possibilities – differential remedial and 'treatment' programmes for the non-attenders of each category and the possibility of advancement in studies into the relationship between personality and absenteeism (see Chapter 7).

On the basis of my own preliminary research, I consider that the traits depicted by each group will include the following:

The Traditional or Typical Absentee
The Traditional or Typical Absentee follows the earlier description of the truant offered by Tyerman (1968)./Thus, Traditional Absentees may be isolates who come from an unsupportive home background, possibly with a tendency to be shy/ It is likely that they will have a low self-concept (Reid, 1982a), be introverted and the victim of their social circumstances. By nature, Traditional Absentees will be pleasant when spoken to and liable to acquiesce rather than to search for confrontation. They may well be aware of their own social and educational limitations and so seek compensation by insulating themselves from the unrewarding stimuli at school – just like Billy Casper in *Kes*.

The Institutional Absentee
Institutional Absentees miss school purely for educational reasons. Unlike Traditional Absentees, they may be extraverts, engage in confrontation and, indeed, may even remain on the school premises although out of lessons. Institutional Absentees are more likely to indulge in 'on the spur of the moment' absences from lessons and be selective about days or lessons to miss. They often have a higher self-concept than Traditional Absentees and have quite large numbers of friends. Institutional Absentees may even be the leaders of groups of absentees, have a complete disregard for authority and be unconcerned about the outcome of any punitive measures taken against them. Like Traditional Absentees, they are likely to come from deprived and/or unsupportive home backgrounds. It is probable that some Institutional Absentees will have 'matured' on a diet of squabbles at home, in their immediate neighbourhood and in their classrooms.

The Psychological Absentee
Psychological Absentees miss school mainly for psychological or psychological-related factors such as illness, psychosomatic complaints, laziness, a fear of attending school for any reason (such as dislike of a teacher, a lesson, an impending confrontation or fear of bullying) or because of other physical or temperamental disadvantages, like handicaps or tantrums. Psychological Absentees probably need specialist counselling or skilled as well as empathetic pastoral care to help them to overcome their justified or irrational fears or prejudices.

49

The Generic Absentee

The Generic Absentee is the pupil who misses school for two or three of the above reasons, either simultaneously or over a longer period.

Implications for Practitioners

Teachers need to understand that it is dangerous to generalise in applying common 'causal' traits to individual absentees. Every absentee requires a tailor-made approach. Even more important, teachers and school administrators must realise that the decisions they take can affect attendance in their institution and the quality of the lives of some of their most at-risk pupils. Much more thought needs to be given to the way pupils select their curriculum options particularly in the third or fourth year of secondary education when entrants to external examinations are finalised. More imagination is needed in the way form teachers are selected for classes which contain a large number of absentees as a good relationship between form tutors and pupils at risk is essential in breaking down barriers. Likewise, it is wrong that lower ability forms in secondary schools tend to be taught by the weakest or least well qualified staff more often than their able counterparts. Some thought also needs to be given to whether all lessons should be compulsory for all pupils. For example, is it wise that all pupils must participate in games activities on very cold, wet days? If some young people thought there were alternatives to certain lessons they might attend school more regularly.

Form teachers and staff with pastoral responsibilities need to take great care to ensure that they understand thoroughly all the pupils in their charge. Good teacher/pupil relationships can forestall much absenteeism and, when it occurs, can activate more quickly satisfactory remedial and re-integration schemes. Some teachers make very little attempt to get to know their non-conforming pupils and have no time for them, but, conversely, some staff and school administrators in other institutions argue that they know far more about their deviant than their conformist pupils.

From experience, my own impression is that the general relationship between Institutional Absentees and teachers is not always as good as it might be, possibly because this category contains a number of disruptive and aggressive truants. By contrast, Traditional Absentees frequently reject their schooling but feel less alienated than Institutional Absentees from their teachers and schools because their non-attendance often has different causes. Moreover, Institutional Absentees are often extraverts who display 'couldn't care less' attitudes towards authority whereas Traditional Absentees are introverted pupils who often feel inadequate in crowds, in group activities and in their teacher–pupil relationships. Despite these differences, there is now some evidence to show that some persistent absentees view their teachers less favourably than their parents, even when it is known that some of their teachers (especially form tutors) have tried very hard to help them (Reid, 1983c).

Teachers, therefore, should not expect to achieve miracles with chronic absentees but should, perhaps, settle for much less and not feel deflated when their best endeavours are rejected. Frequently the home and social backgrounds of absentees and truants are so unfavourable that it lies outside the scope of teachers to do more than simply scratch the surface. Sometimes the problems which concern truants require specialist counselling and social work intervention from professionals with access to the appropriate resources.

Teachers, especially those in middle management, should 'train' themselves to heed warning signs which lead to absenteeism. The symptoms are too numerous to list but include factors such as lateness to lessons or school in the morning, a lengthy illness, a change of class, dissatisfaction with curriculum options and an unsatisfactory teacher–pupil relationship.

There is no reason why more schools and teachers should not undertake their own 'market research' into the reasons pupils do not attend school or miss certain lessons. This information may provide valuable clues to pupils' problems as well as indicating some of the measures, preventative and remedial, which the schools need to take in order to combat the problem of non-attendance.

The reasons for pupil non-attendance are generally well known, indeed, they have not changed much for generations. But what effect the introduction of comprehensive secondary education has had upon local rates of absenteeism is not clear. Some educationists, for example, contend that it has led to an increase in absenteeism but they do not provide evidence to support this view (Boyson, 1974; Reynolds and Murgatroyd, 1977). It may well be that what these critics are really doing is drawing attention to the close link which exists between disaffection and absenteeism. How the precise relationship between disaffection and absenteeism and underachievement and absenteeism is measured will pose difficult problems for researchers to overcome in the years ahead.

5
Social Aspects of Truancy and Absenteeism

A great deal more has been written about the home and social backgrounds of truants and school absentees than any other facet of these two related phenomena. However, some large gaps do remain.

Summary of What is Known

Truants and absentees are likely to originate from:

a   families at the lower end of the social scale – the father is either in unskilled or semi-skilled work (often Groups IV and V of the Registrar General's Classification of Occupations) (Davie *et al.*, 1972; Fogelman and Richardson, 1974; May, 1975; Fogelman *et al.*, 1980);

b   families where paternal unemployment or irregular employment is the norm (Blythman, 1975; May, 1975; Farrington, 1980);

c   families where the father is away from the home for long periods, either for reasons of work (merchant seamen) or other reasons (Hersov, 1960a; Wedge and Prosser, 1973);

d   families on low incomes (Tyerman, 1968; Hodges, 1968; Blythman, 1975; Farrington, 1980; Galloway, 1982);

e   families where maternal unemployment, inability to find work, or full or part-time employment in low income occupations is rife (Reid, 1984a);

f   families with an above average number of children (Brooks *et al.*, 1962; Mitchell, 1972);

g   families living in overcrowded conditions (Tyerman, 1968; Fogelman *et al.*, 1980);

h   families living in poor and/or old housing, frequently council or rented rather than privately owned (Tibbenham, 1977);

i   families overcoming or experiencing marital disharmony such as parental divorce or separation (Elliott, 1975; Hodges, 1968; Tyerman, 1968; Scottish Education Department, 1977);

j   one parent families (Ferri, 1976);
k   poor material conditions within the home (Tyerman, 1968; May, 1975; Tibbenham, 1977; Farrington, 1980);
l   families where the parents are unable to cope with a single or variety of social pathologies which threaten their life styles and lead to abnormal conditions within the home: these include alcoholism (Scottish Education Department, 1977; SASD, 1977; Strathclyde Regional Council, 1977), mental (Galloway, 1980a) and physical illness (Scottish Education Department, 1977), violence (Farrington, 1980), family disorganisation (Carmichael, 1975) and associated stress factors (Scottish Education Department, 1977);
m   families in which the parents are uncooperative and/or hostile to authority in general, especially to school authorities (Scottish Education Department, 1977);
n   families where the parents are not interested in their children's progress at school (Fogelman and Richardson, 1974; Blythman, 1975 Fogelman *et al.*, 1980);
o   families where the parents do not insist that their children attend school, or take no notice of their absence (Tyerman, 1968; Galloway, 1976b), and/or do not insist on prompt attendance at school as manifested by their children oversleeping, being late and disliking school journeys (ILEA, 1981; Reid, 1982c);
p   families where the children are supplied with free school meals (Galloway, 1976a);
q   families where the parents are passive victims of a dreadful environment and unsure of their constitutional rights (Scottish Education Department, 1977).

As all these conditions have been found to be rife among the social and home backgrounds of truants and absentees, it is clear that these primary- and secondary-aged pupils are at a major disadvantage throughout their schooling. Such pupils, for example, do not normally receive proper parental encouragement and support at home, emanate from backgrounds where books and learning are valued or find themselves provided with the financial back-up necessary to clothe and equip them properly for their education. Moreover, the breadth of these pupils' experiences is often somewhat limited as they are generally less likely to travel around Britain with their parents, visit places of interest or go for holidays abroad.

Bob

Bob exemplifies many of the characteristics mentioned above. He lives with his parents, sister and brothers in semi-squalid conditions in a three-bedroomed council house situated close to a busy industrial estate in a large conurbation. The inside of the house shows signs of advanced decay – bare walls, much dampness and a general level of disrepair. Much of the furniture is old, the low quality carpets are well worn and the tiny garden is uncared for. Bob's father, an unemployed factory worker (formerly a long distance lorry driver), spends much of his time in the home or occupied at a nearby betting shop.

Evidence obtained from reports in his school files shows that, despite low ability, his lack of progress in school is entirely due to his non-attendance which is attributed to circumstances at home. In an average term, he misses about 85 per cent of possible attendances. Bob's parents have been prosecuted for his truancy and fined. ('My mother cares quite a lot – sometimes she cries. I don't think my father is really bothered. He says missing school never did him any harm.')

Psychological measures indicate that Bob has a low academic self-concept and a low level of general self-esteem. His behaviour (when in school) is rated by his form teacher as quite good, although he depicts some neurotic rather than anti-social tendencies. Evidence from the use of a version of Kelly's (1955) repertory grid technique which consists basically of establishing the similarities and dissimilarities which the individual sees between the people and things in his or her life (People Important to Me in Life) suggests that he cares deeply for his parents despite overwhelming evidence that they tend to neglect him – after Bob had been prosecuted for trespassing on a railway line and theft from a local store, a confidential social worker's report suggested that he was a victim of 'gross parental neglect'.

Bob fits the description of the typical, isolated truant who comes from a deprived and unsupportive home background with a low self-concept and little ambition or drive – one of life's failures. He is one of those pathetic absentees whose search for things to do to while away the time when he is away from school has inadvertently led to brushes with the authorities at school and the law. Bob's case is representative of many – children from low income families whose overwhelming social distress exacerbates and interferes with their progress at school due to lack of parental support and being blessed with few of life's natural advantages.

What is Not Known

The opinions which parents have about their children's schooling is a subject about which too little is generally known. Although most parents recognise the fundamental importance of a good start in life and want their children to do well, some seem to be out of touch with modern schooling and make judgements based solely on their own experiences at school.

Many studies have reached the conclusion that parents of truants and absentees tend to display anti-education values. However, these studies have usually relied upon the subjective and perhaps prejudiced views of education welfare officers, amongst others (Stott, 1966), and the children themselves (Bird *et al.*, 1980; Fogelman *et al.*, 1980). Charts of the number of visits made by parents to schools have been drawn (Fogelman and Richardson, 1974; Blythman, 1975; Fogelman *et al.*, 1980) and show that the parents of absentees and truants tend to made fewer visits to schools than the parents of good attenders (see Chapter 10).

However, other studies have suggested that a high proportion of the parents of truants and absentees are interested in the education of their children and that they do not collude in their absence (Mitchell and Shepherd, 1980; Bird *et al.*, 1980). Clear evidence of the disparities which can exist between the views of parents, teachers and pupils is shown in Fogelman's (1976) account of Britain's sixteen year olds. He reported that substantial differences were found in pupils' attendance habits as indicated in the responses made by parents, teachers and the youths themselves.

Thus, the views of the parents of non-attenders and their interest in education as reported in existing studies is too simplistic. Some findings to date merely reflect the evaluation of the situation by teachers, researchers and other third parties, rather than reporting on results obtained from truants and/or their parents. Brown (1983) suggests that the only way to correct this is to stop using indirect methods of gauging parental interest in schooling.

One of the reasons for this omission is that it is not easy for researchers to obtain the requisite permission from local authorities to visit parents in their homes to discuss their children's non-attendance at school. Even if permission is given, the researchers may not receive a warm welcome from either the parents or the pupils. Moreover, the involvement of parents in a study may displease social workers and the schools as such research may interfere with their casework and remedial programmes. It is issues like these which militate against good multi-disciplinary studies taking place – precisely the sort of work which is urgently required if real progress is to be made to combat and overcome persistent non-attendance from school.

Implications for Practitioners

Despite the overwhelming evidence that truants and absentees tend to come from unfavourable and unsupportive home and social backgrounds, not all pupils from such backgrounds miss school. At best, therefore, these social aspects are but one part – albeit a very important facet – of a complex, multi-causal and multi-disciplinary problem.

Nevertheless, the fact remains that the links between schools and parents are not always as good or as effective as they might be. Good school/parent relationships can forestall and prevent much absenteeism. When schools can get parents on to their side the battle is half won. Regrettably this is unusual, especially as so much casework with non-attenders and their parents is retrospective and punitive in nature. This often leads to an impasse which in turn tends to exacerbate rather than reduce conflict between the two factions. Liaison between education welfare officers, schools, parents and the social services is not always as good as it should be – another factor contributing to breakdowns in the communication process. Much more thought needs to be given to these matters as the best results are usually obtained through hard work and co-operation. This is an aspect into which further research is urgently needed.

Returning to a more basic level, parents' evenings in schools should be arranged at realistic times in the year. Too many take place at or towards the end of academic years when much of the valuable information imparted is of little use – especially when form and subject teachers do not rotate with the year groups.

Poor communication between staff within schools, as well as inadequate pupil record systems, militate against effective measures for combatting or controlling absenteeism in many institutions. For instance, it is common practice in some schools to prevent form and subject teachers from having direct access to all or part of pupils' records. Often confidential records are located separately from the remainder which means that many teachers are not party to information given by educational psychologists and social workers. Moreover, education welfare officers often tend to impart verbal information solely to middle management rather than form and/or subject teachers. In either case, teachers in the classroom are excluded from the diagnostic and remedial process when they are the very people most likely to come into early contact with the absentees. People in authority should not be surprised, therefore, when staff inadvertently carry out different policies and practices from those which are needed in the prevailing situation.

Such basic failures in communication are easily remedied. One way is to put non-confidential information on selected sections of the staff notice-board. Another is to organise a school absentee bulletin which is given to staff on a weekly basis. These measures are relatively inexpensive, except in terms of time, and they have the merit of keeping all staff up-to-date with the latest developments.

Finally, both primary and secondary schools need to do a great deal more to identify and help those pupils who are deemed to be most at risk as a result of their social, home and environmental circumstances. Sadly, without such early identification, certain at-risk pupils are liable to graduate to absenteeism, truancy, maladjustment and/or delinquency well before the appropriate social and school agents have responded. When this happens, many professionals will find they have arrived on the scene too late and are fighting a lost cause.

6

Social and Psychological Aspects

The Malaise in Teaching

Without doubt there is a major problem of disenchantment and disaffection amongst pupils in many secondary schools in Britain, but the relationship between this disaffection and truancy is not known. Nevertheless, substantial numbers of youngsters do feel alienated from both their schools and the type of education which they receive (see Chapters 9–12). Clearly, if more non-attenders felt happier about the process of schooling, presumably they would attend school regularly.

Similarly, a large number of teachers are disenchanted with their job – some even dislike it. Although this malaise is unmeasurable, it is, and has been, apparent to those within the education service for some time. Many people seem to think that this malaise has a simple root cause emanating from the changes which have taken place over the last twenty years in teachers' professional attitudes towards their status, role and duties. It is argued that the denigration of teaching from a vocational to a task-orientated profession has led to an increase in apathy throughout the system. This, in turn, is supposed to have led to a decrease in public and pupil esteem for the teaching profession. Some people now believe that this malaise is spreading a malignant cancer throughout the education service, fuelled by such factors as over-large schools and class sizes, recent cut-backs in the amount of money spent on schools, teachers, equipment and textbooks, changes in the curriculum and employment opportunities, as well as significant changes in the organisation, structure and management of schools. The combatting of this dangerous malaise is one of the greatest challenges facing today's educationists.

Nor is this situation peculiar to Britain. In a study undertaken in the Irish Republic, Raven (1975) concluded that many teachers tend to live in a state of 'pluralistic ignorance' about their pupils' priorities, aspirations and wishes, the contributions of their colleagues and the requirements of the pupils' parents. He suggested that too many teachers are examination-orientated and totally unaware that a high proportion of the pupils in their schools are bored (see also Fogelman, 1976).

In this respect, the recent school differences research of Reynolds *et al.*

(1976) and Rutter *et al.* (1979) (see Chapter 8) is encouraging as their work has shown that to some extent schools have it in their own hands to combat these worrying trends. The practices and policies which schools adopt can and do make substantial differences to the level of disaffected behaviour manifested by pupils, as well as to the *quality* of pupils' educational experiences. Whether this message is fully understood by teachers, administrators and policy-makers must remain an open question.

No doubt, many people will be dubious on this issue, given the uncertainty of human nature. Others may be justifiably cynical. For example, Mullen's (1950) findings led to few changes in the attitudes of teachers towards such disenchanted pupils as truants and absentees. He reported then that the correlates of good attendance are rewarding, profitable school experiences like good grades, teacher approval, participation in extra-curricular activities, high character ratings and favourable home circumstances. He showed that poor attenders are characterised by such traits as lower grades, general disaffection from school, home illnesses, fewer aids at home and at school and less teacher approval.

What difference is there today? Probably none. And yet, as the resource implications of remedial action are so slight and so little improvement is evident over a considerable span of time, the prognosis for enlightened change in the foreseeable future is relatively bleak. The leads given by Reynolds and Rutter could well be destined to fall on stony ground unless the influence of HM Inspectorate – through the publication of their school visitation reports – have long-, as well as short-term effects.

The Labelling of Non-attenders

Far more thought needs to be given by teachers to the way they talk about non-conforming pupils in schools. Too many teachers fail to realise that the consequences of labelling less able and disadvantaged pupils as 'delinquent', 'maladjusted' and 'truant' can be counter-productive. It seems that once certain pupils know they have been unfavourably categorised, they soon learn to appreciate the difficulties involved in changing their teachers' unfavourable perceptions of them.

Research workers who have studied the problem (Hargreaves *et al.*, 1975) have been able to give valuable insights into the attitudes of deviant pupils in education. For example, in the United States, Shelton's (1976) study of juvenile non-attendance from school showed that many labels given by teachers to so-called deviant pupils are inappropriate and can be unhelpful given the complicated social and educational backgrounds of the pupils themselves. Too often, it appears, teachers tend to use emotive terms like 'delinquent' and 'truant' as convenient labels irrespective of whether or not these are appropriate to the particular behaviour. Many teachers simply refer to all non-attendance as 'truancy' irrespective of cause. The contest facing educationists is to protect the individual child from invidious, often incorrect, labels while at the same time keeping public attention focused on the requirements of those children with special educational needs.

Personal Characteristics of Non-attenders

West (1982) undertook a systematic, longitudinal study of some 411 young males recruited at the age of eight from six state primary schools in a working-class area of London and followed up to the age of 25, by which time a third of the group had acquired a criminal record. The aim of the work was to obtain a better understanding of the reasons why youngsters become delinquents. The findings, reported by both West (1982) and Farrington (1980), show that high delinquency-rate schools usually have correspondingly poor attendance rates.

Five point nine per cent of the pupils were identified by their teachers as truants in their primary schools. This is about twice the percentage obtained from the National Child Development study (Fogelman and Richardson, 1974) and the Isle of Wight survey (Rutter *et al.*, 1970) but as West's work contained such a high proportion of children from urban and working-class backgrounds, this is hardly surprising. Seventeen point five per cent and 17.8 per cent of the boys respectively were found to be self-reported or teacher-reported truants at the age of 14. However, these totals were respectively lower and higher at the ages of 12 and 16, which conforms well with the tendency for pupils' truancy to increase with age.

The research shows that the most significant predictor of truancy from secondary school is a rating of pupils as troublesome by primary teachers and their peers. In other words, pupils who reveal behavioural problems of one kind or another in primary schools are more likely than their counterparts to become truants at some point in their secondary school careers.

More than a third of the truants were found to have originated from the following backgrounds: families with low incomes; large families; slum housing; criminal parents; poor parental child-rearing behaviour; marital disharmony; poor parental supervision; and enforced separations from their parents for one reason or another. The truants also tended at the age of 11 to have low intelligence quotients, poor vocabulary and poor primary school-leaving reports. Over a quarter came from low social class backgrounds, had delinquent siblings, fathers with erratic job records and parents with a low interest in education.

At the primary stage, the truants were found to lack concentration, to be restless, to be more difficult to discipline, to care little about their parents' attitudes towards their behaviour and to be untidy or unclean on arrival at school. At the secondary stage, the teachers' assessments worsened and the number of negative features displayed by the truants increased. These now included laziness, untidiness in class work, lack of concern about being a credit to parents and lack of concentration, as well as being restless in class and disobedient, difficult to discipline, unduly resentful after criticism or punishment, quarrelsome and aggressive, and inclined to show off and seek attention, tell lies to keep out of trouble and persistently to be late.

Not surprisingly, a large proportion of the truants were found to have low positions in class and to be poor readers. Other traits found among some of the truants included anxious dispositions, tendencies to day-dream, to be tired and washed-out, to be ignored by other children, to be gloomy and sad, diffident about competing with other children and unable to make friends.

Farrington (1980), in analysing the characteristics of the truants in West's sample, noted that many of the results quoted in relation to truancy mirror results previously published in relation to delinquency. Background features such as large family, low income, other delinquents in the family, unsatisfactory upbringing, disharmony between parents and early troublesomeness were similar. As young adults both the truants and the delinquents showed a similar tendency to be anti-social. West concludes that '. . . to be concerned about delinquents means that one must also be concerned about truants'.

The published findings of both West and Farrington accord well with previous work. Various studies have reported that a high proportion of truants of secondary age tend to be liars (Hersov, 1960a), to be nevous and aggressive (Douglas *et al.*, 1968), and to suffer from inconsistent home discipline (Hersov, 1960a), including the frequent use of corporal punishment by parents (Tyerman, 1968).

Studies conducted on children of primary school age have, according to their teachers (May, 1975), found truants and school absentees to be lazy (Douglas and Ross, 1965), liars, bullies, disobedient, miserable, worriers, and often unpopular with peers and teachers alike.

Cooper (1966) has reported that many truants have less well developed physiques than their peers. Farrington's work only partially supports Cooper's as he found that while truants are likely to be relatively small between the ages of eight and ten, height was not a factor related to truancy at the age of 14, and weight was an unrelated factor at either eight to ten or 14.

By the ages of 14 and 16, Farrington found that over a quarter of truants could be classified as neurotic extraverts. By contrast, Kavanagh and Carroll (1977), using a different but related inventory, reported that poor attenders are high on neuroticism but average on extraversion (see also Reid, 1984b, and the section on personality and absenteeism on page 71ff.).

Farrington found that there was no significant tendency for truants to be rated unpopular by their peers at the ages of eight to ten. However, Croft and Grygier's (1956) work on teacher-rated secondary school truants found that they were rated unpopular by both teachers and classmates. It may well be, therefore, that the attitudes of teachers and peers significantly harden, and polarise in some instances, as the truants get older, not only because of their non-attendance and lack of interest in school, but also because of a number of related traits such as lying, laziness, solitariness, as well as their generally unfavourable attitudes when in school.

Truanting often starts before officially recorded delinquency and so can be used to identify individuals 'at risk' of criminality. Robins and Ratcliff (1980) showed that in their later years in St Louis, former truants had a greatly raised incidence of problems with jobs, alcohol, marriage, crime and violence. A suggestion of similarly adverse long-term sequelae of truancy in Britain comes from the high incidence of former truants among prisoners (Pitts and Simon, 1954).

The National Child Development study data point inexorably to the location of the overwhelming proportion of absenteeism among children of the working class (Fogelman and Richardson, 1974). These statistics also show, not surprisingly, that there is a strong association, regardless of social class, between low school performance and absenteeism. These findings, like work on delinquency, confirm the importance of trying to organise schools to serve the needs of the underprivileged rather better than they appear to be doing at the moment.

Obviously, improving school attendance lessens opportunities for pupils to commit offences. Belson (1975) reports that among London schoolboys, an appreciable amount of stealing takes place during truancy, especially among persistent truants. This would seem to suggest that truancy prevention reduces juvenile crime. Some support for this conclusion is obtained from the work of Frazer (1979) who showed that a successful campaign to reduce school absences was followed by the disappearance of juveniles from the shopping centres in Kilmarnock and a marked decrease in reported shop lifting. Ekblom (1979) has produced evidence that the use of truancy patrols by police in large cities can reduce juvenile crime for up to two weeks after each single week of patrolling. West (1982) suggests, however, that the benefits of enforced attendance by means of police patrols to round up truants, or by a more vigorous policy of prosecutions by education welfare officers, are likely to be short term unless the root causes of pupil alienation are tackled simultaneously.

Intelligence

Several researchers have noted a link between truancy and attainment (Hersov, 1960a; Cooper, 1966; Douglas *et al.*, 1968; Rutter *et al.*, 1970, 1979; Fogelman and Richardson, 1974; May, 1975; Farrington, 1980). Indeed, over fifty years ago, Dayton (1928) noted that '. . . the most important contributing factors [to truancy] are the school, the neighbourhood, and the home, together with the individual make-up of the child, which may include mental deficiency'.

While low intelligence may be a contributory factor in truancy, it is not the sole cause of dropping out of school as most less intelligent pupils attend school willingly and regularly. Furthermore, many truants and absentees may not be innately any less intelligent than their peers; they simply attend school on fewer occasions and so fare worse in standardised and school tests as well as in public examinations.

May (1975) found that at the age of nine plus irregular attenders had statistically significant lower IQ scores than good attenders. His truant group had a mean IQ which was fully 15 points lower than non-truants. Fogelman and Richardson (1974) used general ability and NFER attainment tests on secondary pupils in the National Child Development cohort, and found a significant inverse relationship between absence and test scores for pupils from working-class backgrounds, especially those from unskilled occupations.

Whereas most writers have commented upon the low intelligence of many truants (Tyerman, 1958), the opposite has been reported in several studies conducted on school refusers. According to Model and Shepherd (1958), Chazan (1962), Leventhal and Sills (1964) and Berg (1980), many school refusers have above average to superior intelligence but not all experts agree with this conclusion. For instance, Hampe *et al.* (1973), who studied a large sample, found there to be no difference between school refusers and the general population in terms of the distribution of intelligence. Such confusion has prompted Reynolds and Murgatroyd (1977) to hint that some so-called refusal associated with intelligent and middle-class children is, in fact, truancy, in much the same way as the term 'dyslexia' is freely used with certain pupils from affluent backgrounds who are slow readers. Conversely, it remains possible that some truancy amongst less intelligent and lower class children is, in fact, school refusal. Many educationists have long believed that better remedial provision in schools (especially individual tuition in the basic skills) is one of the best ways to forestall and overcome much truancy and absenteeism (see Ralphson, 1973; Blythman, 1975).

The fact that the relationship between non-attendance and under-achievement is seen as a thorny issue was mentioned in Chapter 9. This relationship is difficult to measure because under-achievement is not something which is simply present or absent, but is a matter of degree (Rutter and Yule, 1976). In Great Britain, most research on under-achievement has concentrated upon reading difficulties, psychiatric disorders and the remedial treatment involved. Generally speaking, educators tend to view truants and many absentees as being academic under-achievers. This is hardly surprising. When a pupil is continually absent, it follows that he or she is more likely to under-achieve and less likely to partake in the continuous developmental programme of experiences and instruction in schools that will meet the pupils' present and later needs in life.

Adjustment Characteristics

There is much to suggest that a small proportion of schoolchildren experience difficulties in adjusting to 'school life', especially during their formative and primary years. However, most children enjoy the life once the continuity is established and simple dislike of school does not seem to be sufficient cause for absenteeism amongst children of primary age.

As they approach adolescence, children's attitudes towards school tend to polarise into the favourable and unfavourable. One view is that certain children with a high incidence of familial neurosis have a tendency to become school refusers (Hersov, 1960a), while children from deprived home and social backgrounds play truant (Tyerman, 1968). This is, of course, a dangerous and misleading over-simplification although certainly, there is a lessening of enthusiasm for school amongst some older children, especially those who feel increasingly alienated from their institutions (Reid, 1981). Transfers of pupils from primary to secondary schools, class promotions and demotions can all precipitate some pupil anxiety, particularly amongst less able pupils, which may or may not lead to absenteeism. Further research on these matters is needed before all the educational implications are properly understood.

Maladjustment and Absenteeism

It is widely believed that all truants are either maladjusted or delinquent but this is not true. Evidence shows that while many truants are unhappy, unsociable and friendless and fail to persevere (Tyerman, 1968), others fall within the 'stable range' (Carroll, 1977b).

It appears that these findings differ according to the way samples of truants are selected. Stott (1966) used his *Bristol Social Adjustment Guides* to show that truants are three times more maladjusted than non-truants from the same neighbourhood. However, the work was undertaken with a 'clinical' sample of truants – children who have been processed to varying degrees by the authorities (social services, educational psychologists, the courts and so on). By contrast, Carroll used a broader sample of Persistent Absentees from a single comprehensive school and found that whilst poor attenders are more maladjusted than good attenders, the differences between the two groups were not statistically significant.

The differences obtained from findings from these same samples can be explained. It seems that there are differences between persistent and occasional truants. For example, Galloway (1980a) compared teacher-assessed truants with truants referred to a psychiatric clinic. He concluded that the latter were far more likely to display an inability to form relationships within school. Indeed, it seems that the inability to form good peer group friendships within school is one sign of maladjustment amongst non-attenders.

Delinquency and Non-attendance

As mentioned earlier in the chapter, the link between delinquency and truancy has long been established (Healy, 1915; Burt, 1925; Hodges, 1968; Tennent, 1971; West and Farrington, 1973; Monroe, 1973; Finlayson and Loughran, 1976; O'Hagan, 1977; Hoghughi, 1978; West, 1982). Like truants, delinquents often come from an unfavourable home background, characterised by multiple adversities, and tend to have anti-social and deviant life styles after leaving school. Farrington (1980) suggests that adverse backgrounds produce anti-social people, and that truancy and delinquency are just two symptoms of this. Farrington's study contradicts the work of Reynolds and Murgatroyd (1977) by showing that secondary schools have no influence on either truancy or delinquency rates. Galloway (1980a) reports that absenteeism rates in comprehensive schools are significantly related to absenteeism rates in their feeder primary schools.

More worrying for teachers is the work of Lalli and Savitz (1976). They found that delinquent behaviour within school can be a major reason for truancy. They reported that in Philadelphia a large percentage of youngsters felt unsafe during the time spent both in and travelling to school and a majority of parents were fearful that their children could be injured or robbed while at school. Although substantial differences still remain between New York and Chicago when compared to their British counterparts in terms of school theft, vandalism and physical attacks carried out on teachers and pupils, many educationists believe that some of these gaps are closing, especially in places like Inner London, Liverpool, Glasgow and many industrial conurbations.

The Behaviour of Persistent Absentees

Until recently, very little specific research had been undertaken into the relationship between absenteeism and school behaviour. My research (reported in 1984b) analysed data obtained from the results of giving the Children's Behaviour Questionnaire (Rutter, 1967) to the form teachers of 77 Persistent Absentees and two control groups over a three-week period.

The pupils came from a large comprehensive school situated in a deprived catchment area in industrial South Wales and the Questionnaire was used to measure the pupils' behaviour and to ascertain their scores for neuroticism and anti-social behaviour.

The findings revealed that the Persistent Absentees displayed significantly more behavioural traits than the pupils in the two control groups with higher levels of neuroticism and anti-social conduct. However, a majority of the Absentees showed no signs of any neurotic or anti-social behaviour (61 and 65 per cent respectively).

A closer inspection of the results revealed that many Absentees had some disorders, such as disobedience, which were not solely confined to their erratic attendance at school. For instance, apart from variables which related directly to truancy, other large differences between the three groups were found on seven items on the Questionnaire. These were: not much liked by other children; tends to do things on his own – rather solitary; often appears miserable, unhappy, tearful or distressed; has poor concentration or short attention span; often tells lies; is often disobedient; and has stolen things on one or more occasions.

Some interesting group and sex differences were found within these data. For example, male rather than female absentees scored higher on both the main Questionnaire and the Anti-social Sub-scale which suggests that male absentees behave more badly in school than their female counterparts. More significantly, both the male and female Absentees' scores were approximately three times as great as the good attenders in both control groups and on most comparisons of the two Sub-scales. These are important results as they suggest that the behaviour of male and female Absentees has more in common with one another than with the behaviour of good attenders. The findings therefore reinforce the need for further research to be undertaken into this complex topic. It may well be that the behaviour of absentees will be worst in those schools which have very poor teacher–pupil relationships.

Disruptive Behaviour and Absenteeism

A great deal of research has been undertaken into the concept of disruption and disruptive behaviour in schools (Lowenstein, 1975; Jones-Davies and Cave, 1976; Laslett, 1977; Lawrence *et al.*, 1977; Bird *et al.*, 1980; Docking, 1980; Tattum, 1982). These studies highlight the importance of several facets on pupil behaviour. These include: unfavourable home backgrounds; the premature acquisition of adult experiences; responsibilities and status at home which makes school appear petty and restrictive; anti-authoritarian and anti-school attitudes fostered in the home and supported by an anti-education neighbourhood culture; homes in which there are serious tensions in familial relationships and/or where parental authority is exercised harshly; and pupils who attend but have no formal interest in school and so consciously decide to subvert any orderly classroom behaviour for their own social or perverse pleasure.

The theory that disruptive behaviour in school is related to truancy and persistent school absenteeism is not new. Interest in this topic is increasing and there have been a number of reports and projects on disruptive behaviour linked to school absenteeism (UCAC, 1975; Educational Institute of Scotland, 1975; Davie, 1980; NAS/UWT, 1981; Galloway *et al.*, 1982; Frude and Gault, 1984). For example, I (Reid, 1984c) cite cases of three disruptive Persistent Absentees and present extracts from selected interviews obtained during my field work which show, like many other studies on disruptive pupils (for example, Tattum, 1982), that the poor attenders blamed their schools and their teachers rather than other aspects for their behaviour in and out of lessons.

Wayne

Wayne, 15, a pupil with a long history of absenteeism and disruptive behaviour in school, has been 'suspended' on four separate occasions including once for striking a teacher and once for 'repeated verbal abuse and foul language in class without provocation'. In addition, he has appeared in court for truancy, theft and trespassing on private property.

Wayne's father has a long history of unemployment following a serious accident at work which left him partially disabled. Except for a small disability pension, child allowance and social security, the family has few means of support, although Wayne's mother has a cleaning job for two hours a day.

A report from a social worker described Wayne as being 'out of control at home. He is constantly in trouble with his neighbours because of his aggressive nature and language. He is widely suspected on the estate of being responsible for more than a little of the considerable vandalism in the neighbourhood.'

At the end of the Children's Behaviour Questionnaire, Wayne's form teacher wrote '. . . it is better for the entire form as well as the staff when he is away. He is a born troublemaker.'

The following extract is indicative of the way Wayne spoke about his school and the staff during several interviews:

WAYNE: '. . . If I had one wish it would be that someone would do Mr X in or I could get my revenge. He's always had it in for me, ever since I first came here. One day he walked into our class and took me down to his office and caned me because he said I started a riot in Miss Y's lesson. He and everyone else knew there were lots of other people involved but it was only me he caned. Always me. Every time he sees me, I know I'm in trouble. I hate him.'

RESEARCHER: 'Wouldn't you say that with your school record he needs to give you special attention?'

WAYNE: 'Maybe. But he's not fair. None of the teachers here are. Once they've got you down as a villain that's the end of it.'

RESEARCHER: 'Then why don't you try and change and reform your conduct in school?'

WAYNE: 'I've tried. Several times. You've no idea what it's like being me. Every day is a problem – at home with my parents, out on the estate and here. Especially here.'

RESEARCHER: 'Surely then you really need to change for your own sake?'

WAYNE: 'I can't.'

RESEARCHER: 'Why not?'

WAYNE: 'I don't know. Maybe it's too late. Anyway I loathe this place. All it's ever got me is trouble. Mr X in particular is always out to get me. He taunts me when I come back to school. He tries to make me say I was away with a cold and produce a sick note. He knows I can't. Can you imagine what it's like in our class? What would be the use of sitting quietly all the time like most of the girls? We never do anything decent. All we ever do is copy from the blackboard or fill in stupid work sheets. And what do we copy? Rubbish. It's just filling in time. I'm better off when I'm not here. At least I don't get caned for that and I don't have to put up with the likes of him [Mr X].'

Implications for Practitioners

Most commentators agree that very few children are disruptive all the time and that most have a good relationship with at least one teacher. Chronic absentees and disruptive pupils, however, generally have poorer teacher–pupil relationships than most.

Docking (1980) shows that pupils prefer teachers who are relatively strict but fair and approachable and who show an interest in them. Teachers who are regarded as 'soft', ineffective, rigid, harsh, uncaring and remote, and who incite physical confrontations, can provoke deep resentment which may lead to indiscipline and disruption.

Attempting to re-integrate non-conforming and disruptive pupils into the norms of school life can be a hazardous exercise. Persuading disruptive absentees to return to school, for example, can lead to stormy scenes of confrontation. Similarly, pupils who are absent themselves from lessons but remain on the school premises do not always welcome being forced to return to their classrooms.

One trap to avoid is giving disruptive pupils 'special' privileges in school (official or otherwise) in order to achieve some degree of success in controlling them. If this happens, some conforming pupils may well be unable to comprehend the differences in standards expected between them and their disenchanted peers and this in turn can lead to a lowering of morale throughout the school. In schools where pupil–teacher confrontation is the norm, constant disputes can lead to a lowering of staff as well as pupil morale.

Teachers need to be able to distinguish between genuine pleas for help from those truants and absentees whose home backgrounds, social and educational circumstances require understanding and positive remedial assistance and those whose non-attendance is but one manifestation of aggressive, anti-social conduct which often lies outside the scope of many of them to counteract. Above all, teachers need to attempt to maintain control in class through empathetic and positive rather than harsh and provocative means. The worst thing teachers can do is to be too weak because this plays into the hands of the 'agents provocateurs' who will thrive on their ineptitude.

7

Psychological Aspects of Truancy

The aim of this chapter, which discusses the psychological aspects of truancy based on the social and psychological features outlined in Chapter 6, is to give teachers enough knowledge of the subject for them to be able to understand when specialist help is needed. Psychological features relating to the guidance of truants are discussed in Chapter 11.

Although it is important that teachers and social workers have a good grasp of the psychological aspects of truancy, it is equally important that they do not inadvertently give themselves greater credit than they deserve on this score. Teachers should always leave 'work' which requires specialist help to the experts.

Early Psychological Theories of Truancy

Early psychologists had some fairly basic ideas about the reasons for truancy. One school of thought viewed truancy as the expression of an innate instinctive urge. Kline (1898), for example, linked truancy and running away with man's roving instincts, likening it to the migratory instincts of animals, and birds. He argued that whereas the latter were initiated by sex urges, man's 'wanderlust spirit' had its origins in the food-seeking habits of his ancestors who, in the hunting and fishing stages of development, were forced to roam in search of food. Kline showed that running away and truancy were more common in spring and summer than in autumn and winter.

Healey (1915) supported Kline's ideas on instinct. He argued, however, that the truancy continuum was very broad and could in some cases be taken as a sign of healthy development in children, especially in adolescents. Later psychologists (Burt, 1925; Andriola, 1943, 1946; Hay, 1945), partly influenced by Freudian theory, viewed truancy as an attempt on the part of children:

a   to escape from real or fancied injuries or from intolerable psychological situations;
b   to avoid the pressures and responsibilities which accompany maturity and adulthood;

c   to retreat from 'normal' intellectual growth brought about by an unstable ego, possibly caused by developmental and psychological traumas.

A significant piece of work in the field of truancy was undertaken by Burt (1925) but doubts have been cast upon its validity. However, Burt reported that truants tended to be passive rather than assertive and argued that their behaviour was related to their intellectual capacity. His ideas now need to be treated with considerable caution but, nevertheless, many of Burt's suppositions make sense. Indeed, some of his views have been confirmed by findings obtained by more recent researchers.

Another researcher whose work in the field of truancy and maladjustment became influential in the fifties and sixties was Denis Stott. Stott (1966) undertook a detailed study of 305 truants selected by 168 education welfare officers throughout Great Britain. As far as was possible, one truant was selected from a primary and one from a secondary school for each region. Two 'controls' were chosen for each truant from within the same school. The first control was a child of the same sex born on the same day as the truant or as near to it as possible. These children were known as the birth-date controls. The second control was chosen from the same neighbourhood as the truant in order to obtain a measure of cultural influences.

Using the *Bristol Social Adjustment Guides*, Stott found that the mean scores for the truants were more than three times higher than those for the neighbourhood and birth-date controls. This meant that 63 per cent of the truants were classified as maladjusted, compared with approximately 10 per cent of the controls. Stott concluded that theories which argued that deviance is the typical behaviour of young people in certain neighbourhoods were without foundation. For example, the scores for some of the controls who lived in the same neighbourhoods as the truants varied little from the birth-date controls.

He also reported that the tolerance thresholds of individual truants and controls varied according to a number of factors. These included: a tendency towards ill health, physical defects, parental interest in education, deprivation, and family size and security.

Stott was one of the first people to question whether truants should be punished for their conduct. Like many more recent writers on truancy, he argued that the traditional remedies of punishment, admonition and fining parents could exacerbate, rather than ease, a situation. Nevertheless, Stott was very strong in his support for the social function of education welfare officers. He suggested that the cost of this service was much less than the expense involved in allowing maladjusted children to form into shiftless, neurotic and/or delinquent sections of the community when they should have been in school.

Stott was a forerunner of the researchers who favour social and psychological approaches to investigate the 'causes' of truancy. The contrast which can now be made between the early temperament, instinct and physical schools, as exemplified in the writings of Kline and Burt, and modern researchers such as Tyerman, Reynolds, Galloway, Rutter and myself is very stark!

Psychological Absence from School

It does not necessarily follow that a pupil is learning or participating in the lessons just because he or she is present in school. An emotional conflict, or lack of interest, are but two factors which can interfere with the continuous learning processes of children. There are undoubtedly vast numbers of pupils in schools who, though physically present, are mentally absent. It is well known that some pupils simply go through the motions of pretending to learn and paying attention in class when, in fact, their minds are on what for them are more stimulating topics, such as football, boy/girl friends and pop music. Lack of pupil interest, irrelevant subject matter and the inability of teachers to project themselves are but three of the many contributing factors to the mass under-achievement and disaffection which currently affect our secondary schools (see Chapter 6, page 62).

Despite the general consensus that this supposition is correct, very little research has been carried out into the processes involved in psychological absence from school, partly because of the methodological difficulties which are inherent in studying the concept. A school of thought, however, still believes it is far better for uninterested, potentially disruptive pupils to let their minds wander than to express their discontent vociferously and so interfere with the progress of their peers!

Introduction to the Latest Research

The research examined in this section is necessarily selective, partly because of the imbalance in the work conducted to date into the relationship between personality factors and non-attendance at school. The section attempts to give the reader broad insights into the work without, given the complexity of the issues, deviating too far into the realms of psychological theory. 'Personality', for example, is a vast field within psychology and many books have been written on it.

Three points must be made here, however. Psychologists often interpret the term 'personality' differently from the majority of people. To the general public, 'personality' simply tends to mean being outgoing, lively and interesting. To be lacking in personality implies the opposite. Someone who is regarded as lacking personality is often seen as being a poor companion. Psychologists, however, emphasise that everyone has personality – some people merely manifest certain traits more than others (extraversion–introversion). For them, the emphasis is upon understanding people rather than making social judgements about them.

Second, personality is situation-specific rather than stable. Children or adults may respond to something in one way with someone they like and quite another with someone they don't, leaving the respondents to draw opposite conclusions. Likewise, children or adults can display high self-esteem on the football field and low self-esteem in maths lessons due to such facets as interest and ability.

Third, similar constraints apply in the two sections on anxiety and absenteeism (page 72) and on the relationship between the self-concept and absenteeism (pages 72–4), especially as anxiety, for instance, is but one of the many contributory elements which go to make up the total personality. Thus, one pupil might have a high score on anxiety and a low one on self-concept, while another shows exactly the opposite traits. In this respect, total scores derived from personality 'tests'/inventories are merely convenient vehicles for researchers and psychologists rather than definitive outcomes (see Reid, 1982a, 1984b).

Personality and Truancy

Until the late 1970s, few projects undertaken on or with truants or absentees had included personality variables or 'tests' in their research designs. Consequently, only general statements about personality tended to be found. These ranged from Tyerman's (1958) investigation, which depicted the truants as likely to be 'lonely', 'unhappy', and 'insecure', to Hersov's (1960a) school refusal study which described this condition as a psychoneurotic personality disorder.

Billington (1979) undertook an analysis of the personality characteristics as measured by a selection of standardised tests of groups of truants and non-truants in four comprehensive schools. He found that truants were much less popular than non-truants, but personality differences in terms of anxiety and insecurity, although present, were not statistically significant. Billington concluded that standard personality inventories may not be sensitive enough to detect the subtle personality differences which may exist between truants and non-truants. He is, surely, partially right in this respect, especially as people are beginning to realise that it is wrong to lump all truants/absentees together in one large group when there are clear differences between various types of non-attenders (see Chapter 4, pages 48–50). Then again, Billington's findings may, in fact, be attributed to the instruments which he used. More 'sensitive' instruments, such as the Repertory Grid (Kelly, 1955) and measures of self-concept, as well as other instruments so far unused with non-attenders, like the 'locus of control' and semantic differentials (Cohen, 1976), can or may lead to more productive results being achieved.

a Anxiety and Non-attendance

The relationship between school refusal and anxiety has long been established (Estes *et al.*, 1956; Coolidge *et al.*, 1964). A related problem, a general fear of going to school without this ever reaching the phobic stage, has also been the subject of a great deal of research at the nursery, primary and secondary stages. Children are particularly reluctant when they first begin voluntary or compulsory education in nursery or infant sections – ask most mothers. Sympathetic support from parents and teachers has been found to be a key variable in helping children to overcome their worries (Bauer, 1980). Starting school is bound to seem strange to young children used to being at home every day.

Likewise, it is only natural that a large percentage of children should prefer to be at home or out playing than at school. If there is any doubt on this score, just listen to the tone of conversation or look at the facial expressions on many pupils at the end of any school term. Despite these preferences most children and teachers turn up at school willingly and inwardly accept the social and educational advantages of regular attendance. Indeed, some children and teachers appear to prefer being at school to being at home (without ever being considered 'workaholics') as a number of people will willingly testify in the long summer holidays.

From time to time, many children from a variety of social and educational backgrounds develop a fear of either attending school or failing once there. This is only normal. Factors contributing to this syndrome can include: the type of work being undertaken, school transfers, demotions, promotions, new or different teachers, teaching styles and subjects, changes in the curriculum, dislike or fear of a particular member of staff or punishment of some kind, bullying, extortion, speaking out aloud in class and many others. Sometimes irrational fears about going to school can be reinforced by illness, falling behind in schoolwork, the failure to complete homework or do it well, unpopularity with peers, inability to participate in or do well at an activity (such as games, swimming, art, drama, music), as well as the failure to wear or have a school uniform. Much depends on the age, sex, ability and temperament of the child but such fears are usually short-lived and overcome by teachers and parents alike without too much difficulty.

An interesting corollary on this theme has been proposed by Withrington (1975). He suggests that while anxiety can play a part in some absenteeism from school, it is the authorities and not the students who generally exhibit this trait. It is, after all, the authorities who have to uphold the law and ensure that children attend school regularly.

b The Self-concept and Non-attendance

Until the early 1980s, a minimum of research on the precise relationship between non-attendance at school and children's self-concepts had been carried out. Working from leads obtained from my social anthropological approach, I (Reid, 1982a) used the Brookover *et al.* (1967) Self-concept of Academic Ability Scale and the shortened form of the Coopersmith (1967) Self-esteem Inventory with 77 Persistent Absentees and two control groups in a large comprehensive school in South Wales.

The findings showed the Persistent Absentees had statistically significant lower self-concepts than the pupils in the two control groups (see Introduction, page 2) as measured by these instruments. There were no significant gender differences between the male and female Absentees although there were highly significant inter-group differences to be found between the male Absentees when compared with the male pupils in each of the two control groups and between the female Absentees and the females in the two control groups. These findings suggest that, like behaviour (Reid, 1984b), taken collectively, Absentees have more in common with one another (whether male or female) than with good attenders.

A closer inspection of the findings obtained when using the Brookover Scale revealed that the Absentees rated themselves as having much less ability than their peers in the two control groups. They also thought they had less chance of entering a professional occupation when they left school and they rated their own work lower than the pupils in the two control groups, irrespective of how the teachers marked their work.

The Coopersmith Scale showed that the greatest differences between the Persistent Absentees and the two control groups were found on six items. The Absentees had a tendency to say things like: 'There are lots of things about myself I'd change if I could'; 'It's pretty tough to be me'; 'Things are all mixed up in my life'; 'I often feel upset in school'; 'I often get discouraged in school'; 'I can't be depended on'.

The implications of these findings are that the Absentees recorded lower scores than the two control groups because they had become more accustomed to patterns of failure at home and at school than their regularly attending peers. It is possible that consistent patterns of failure in school might lead some pupils to withdraw from the offending stimuli. For example, when pupils perpetually receive low grades in school, their academic self-concepts may be reduced to such a point that to absent themselves from school becomes a source of relief. These findings suggest that teachers need to give more thought to the way in which they mark their pupils' work in schools. This could be particularly important for potentially at-risk pupils who are known to come from deprived and unsupportive backgrounds.

To some extent, the findings reinforce the earlier work of Hargreaves (1967) which showed that schools are a more rewarding place for academic pupils than for those in the lower streams. This conclusion is supported by the fact that both the Absentees and their matching controls from the same forms had lower self-concepts than the academic pupils in Control Group 2.

It is not easy to suggest why there were statistically significant differences between the academic self-concepts and general levels of self-esteem of the Absentees and Control Group I pupils who came from identical forms. It seems that the self-concepts of the Control Group I pupils were also adversely affected by regular patterns of failure in school – even if not to the same extent as those of the Absentees.

Nevertheless, these findings can be explained. Presumably, as the Control Group I pupils were attending school regularly, they were receiving positive reinforcement from their schools and homes alike, despite the fact that the occupational status of their parents and their housing and general home circumstances were lower and less favourable than the Control Group 2 pupils. It is probably significant, for example, that the Control Group I pupils had more friends in their particular form and the school as a whole than the Absentees.

What these results mean is that the self-esteem of the Persistent Absentees appeared to be more adversely affected by negative reinforcement than by positive reinforcement than that of pupils in both control groups. Self-esteem, however, is always relative: some Persistent Absentees scored higher than some controls on both Scales, although this trend was far more marked on the Coopersmith Scale. As a result, these data suggest that it is not just the social and educational backgrounds of absentees which make them miss school but also something from within – presumably temperamental and personality factors.

Life-styles of Absentees

I (1983c) decided to use Kelly's (1955) Repertory Grid technique with a one in three sample of the 128 non-attenders in my study in order to uncover original data on the individual 'lives' and 'problems' of a group of Persistent Absentees.

To illustrate the overall findings, potted social and educational histories of Alan and Diane are presented. These summaries indicate the type of data that was collected.

Alan
Alan's parents were divorced when he was eleven years old. Since that time, his home circumstances have deteriorated. Following the divorce Alan, his mother and sister were forced to sell their home in order to go and live on a nearby council estate. Despite all the efforts of Alan's mother, she has never been able to obtain regular employment. Consequently, her only means of support are provided by way of maintenance order, supplementary and child benefits.

During one of his interviews, Alan admitted that he had never been able to accept the finality of his parents' divorce. At one point he made the following revealing statement: 'I get nasty if I see my father around town. When I get home, I seem to shout at everything and everyone. . . .' In fact,

Alan rarely sees or visits his father for a variety of reasons, including lack of paternal interest.

Alan's records show that since the divorce, his behaviour in school has drastically deteriorated. In 1977, he was excluded from school for the first time after 'receiving the cane for a serious offence'. On another occasion, a social worker found him 'mitching' at home with a 'few marks on his legs'. Her confidential report spoke of 'victimisation for unknown reasons by an unknown source – a case to be watched'.

The education welfare officer believes that Alan's mother wants her son to attend school regularly. He feels, however, that she is 'too weak to really do anything about it'. Privately, he considers that Alan's mother is grateful for the company of her son as she leads a very quiet existence. After one of the education welfare officer's visits to the home, Alan claimed that his mother had shaken him continually and told him that he mustn't miss school again. Apart from this, there is no evidence of any further action ever having been taken.

Throughout his interviews, Alan was convivial but pale and badly dressed. In appearance, he is tall and 'gangly' with a mass of pimples and uncombed hair. Mentally, Alan often appeared to be preoccupied and distressed. Sometimes it was difficult to communicate with him.

There can be little doubt that Alan's home circumstances have had and are having an adverse effect upon his progress in school both socially and academically. Prior to the divorce, Alan's performance in school was officially described as 'slow but consistent' by his form teacher. Two years after the divorce, Alan was reported as being 'sullen, deceitful, lazy and a dreadful attender' by a different form teacher. On the same report, the headmaster commented that '. . . he is unlikely to achieve anything until he starts to attend school regularly. His attendance this year has been shocking and I must say that I think he is being very foolish.'

An examination of Alan's Grid shows the very high esteem in which he still holds his father, despite the divorce. The subsequent trauma of life at home without his father has proved a stumbling block which he has been unable to face or overcome either at home or at school. It is also clear that he sees his teachers as being 'dominating', 'strict' and 'showing off' while at the same time, paradoxically, he considers them to be 'helpful'.

Diane

Diane's childhood was enormously complicated. She was born illegitimately, one of seven children including stepbrothers and stepsisters. By the age of fifteen, she had had two stepfathers, both of whom had subsequently divorced her mother. In addition, throughout her childhood Diane experienced a number of unfortunate traumas. On one occasion in her early teens, for example, she was 'placed with her grandmother for safety' on the advice of a social worker. On another, Diane's general practitioner expressed his serious concern about her 'psychological welfare' after she had voluntarily been to see him because she claimed she was having a 'nervous breakdown'. After the visit, the doctor reported Diane's circumstances to the social services. This eventually led to a multi-disciplinary conference being called to discuss her plight. The confidential report written at the time referred to Diane as a 'mental cruelty case'.

At various points during the field work, Diane gave a succession of reasons for her non-attendance at school. These included: 'Mainly because my parents didn't care whether I went to school or not'; 'Because my elder sister didn't go to school'; 'Because I was frightened of the teachers'. In fact, Diane's history of absenteeism began in her primary school. Despite having a reasonable IQ, she received a number of adverse reports on her behaviour during her earliest school-days. For example, a succession of comments on her primary school report referred to her as having frequent bouts of unruly conduct and being a poor attender. Diane claimed that she missed school the first time because of the jibes of some of the other children in her form. She said that they made detrimental remarks about her personal circumstances at home which offended and upset her. Diane's childhood was punctuated by deprivation and uncertainty at home and by hostility and confrontation at school.

The really significant point about Diane's case (like so many others in the study) is that she makes allowances for her home circumstances but not for her teachers. This trend is highlighted by the following statements which she made at various points during the field work.

FIRST STATEMENT: 'All the teachers are very distant from me. They've got to share their feelings with so many other pupils that they haven't got any time for one person. . . . I dislike most of the teachers. They're all the same. They're all mad on the use of the word 'good'. Be 'good' in class. Be a 'good' attender. Be a 'good' girl. They don't believe you're a real person . . . that you can have real problems. They fail to understand your feelings. They don't care. All they think about is themselves and their work. Nothing else matters . . . it's always your fault – never theirs. When I was away from school and missed my exams they all blamed me – none of them even bothered to ask me why I had been away [a note showed she was supposed to have had 'flu]. They all assumed I had done it on purpose. . . .'

SECOND STATEMENT: 'I hate school. Even when I come to school I hate it. There's nothing about it which can make me like it. . . . The teachers don't speak to you unless they're shouting at you. . . . If you explain something to them they just get angry. . . . What they say goes. Some teachers remind me of what Hitler must have been like. . . . Nothing you can say or do matters. . . . It's only them. . . .'

THIRD STATEMENT: 'Teachers should be more like social workers and try to help you. What more can I say? They just don't know how to treat children as people. Schools should change. There should be more facilities at break and lunch-times. . . . There should be less favouritism. . . . Teachers only speak to the 'A' bands, not the 'C' bands . . . the way they treat the 'C' band children is terrible.'

The most revealing feature of Diane's Grid is the dichotomy between the constructs chosen to describe her mother and her teachers. For example, the key constructs chosen to describe the teachers were: 'strangers', 'poor communicators', 'outsiders', 'unable to take a joke', 'uncaring', 'remote', and 'untrustworthy'. By contrast, her mother was described as 'kind', 'lovely', 'beautiful' and 'caring'.

Alan and Diane provide fairly typical examples of the various social, educational and psychological circumstances of absentees and truants. In no way do they represent the worst cases. What their profiles aptly highlight is the link between some of the social, psychological and institutional factors in the lives of individual absentees about which we currently have too little information. The general picture which emerges is one of a struggle for identification, survival and affection both at home and at school.

Implications for Practitioners

The findings reported in this chapter are in some ways less important than are their implications for teachers, social workers and educational psychologists. If it could be proved that raising absentees' and truants' self-concepts (as and when necessary) would lead to an improvement in their attendance, or forestall certain at-risk pupils from starting to miss school, then a considerable step forward would have been taken. My own view is that one way to change and overcome the attitudes of *certain* absentees towards their schools and schooling is to raise their self-concepts. But how can this be achieved?

The simple and pessimistic answer is with difficulty, given the present organisation and ethos of schools. Many schools are simply not in the business of helping those who have rejected the aims and objectives which they are offering. It is a paradoxical situation. The responsibility for raising the self-concepts of pupils involved in illegal actions rests with agents of an institution which the truants have already rejected. So the prognosis for such intervention, unless sensitively handled, is that conflict is likely especially as potential and hardened truants require understanding not coercion.

Let us consider briefly a statement made by Jason, a notorious fourteen-year-old truant from a large comprehensive school in South Wales.

'I guess I just gave up in the end. Every time I came to school, I got told off about my appearance, behaviour and work. . . . Someone would send for me and tell me off again, usually threaten me if I didn't improve I'd be suspended. Then I'd go back to class and be told off for the same things again. . . . Then it was my work. I'd got so far behind in everything, but nobody said let me help you catch up. It was just 'carry on' all the time. When I stayed at home, I was in trouble with my mother. In the end, I gave up. Nobody seemed to understand me or care. I decided the best thing I could do was to go to the park and meet my mates – regular like. At least they were having the same problems. I wanted to learn – but couldn't. Finally, we all said we'd never go back to school but keep one another company instead. Life seemed less of a problem after that . . . at least for a while. . . . Then the Boardy-man called at our house and told my mother that if I didn't go back to school, she'd have to go to court. That night my father shouted at me like never before. After that, I tried to go back to school, but I kept being told off and getting Ds and Es. Well, that's how it is all the time. I try to come so as not to have to go back to court. But when I do, it's a waste of time. I'm in a kind of trap. . . . No one ever helps me.'

Jason's case is not unusual. Empirical evidence suggests that many persistent absentees feel extremely sad about their plight, almost as if they are trapped in some kind of truancy-syndrome. Once they start to stay away, they get further and further behind in their school work and it becomes progressively more difficult for them to return to school – even after the original 'thrill' of deliberately skipping school has vanished. When teachers are unsympathetic to the needs of truants, it is likely that they will inadvertently reinforce the initial deviant conduct which they are trying to overcome. Better teacher–pupil relationships are absolutely essential if the self-esteem of truants is to be raised.

Schools and teachers need to develop new enlightened policies if they are going to combat successfully truancy in their institutions and many will have to change their overt negative attitudes towards truants. They have to be prepared to devise more individual treatment programmes for truants. These schemes should be practical, sympathetic and therapeutic. Such programmes should make it much easier for truants to return to their schools on a regular basis without the risk of further conflict as soon as they enter the school building.

Some of these measures could be quite simple – personal tutor schemes (the choice of person is critical), additional help with reading and writing, sympathetic exclusion from certain lessons, bonus schemes for good attendance and general encouragement and praise whenever an opportunity arises. I have known all these schemes to be successful, especially on a short-term basis (see Chapter 11) but unfortunately, these suggestions are not welcomed in every quarter as they place the onus firmly on to the shoulders of the staff in schools.

The ideas are not new. Their value has already been recognised in previous studies on deviant groups. The Home Office Research Unit (1976), for example, proposed courses on 'Self-concept Therapy' to give girls in trouble more self-respect and confidence.

Likewise Hamblin (1977, 1978) has argued that if schools are to begin to combat and eradicate persistent school absenteeism, then they need to start to understand and eliminate those processes which build and foster negative identities in pupils and which reinforce avoidance behaviour. This means that different types of illegitimate absence require different strategies. School policies need to be flexible, finding the right solution for each individual pupil. There are unlikely to be any overall solutions although some ideas are discussed in later chapters.

There is no doubt that many absentees make clear-cut distinctions between their parents and their teachers, unfavourable to the latter. This seems to happen even when confidential social reports show that individual absentees have been ill or badly treated at home. The Absentees' responses suggest that they see their teachers as being very different from their parents. While it is possible that some absentees make favourable responses about their parents because of the natural loyalties which are commonly associated with family ties, it is interesting that the teachers do not receive the same benefit of the doubt. Teachers, social workers and educational psychologists are outsiders; parents are insiders. This shows the great skill which professionals have to employ if successful outcomes are to be achieved. If teachers want to gain credibility with truants, then they may have to be prepared to take considerable interest in an individual truant over a fairly long period. Truants must feel confident that they can trust the professional to deal with their 'problems' in as empathetic manner as possible. It is not easy to acquire this skill without a great deal of thought and hard work.

Unfortunately, the findings obtained from the repertory grids show another equally important dimension. There was a tendency for all teachers in the school to be tarred by the same brush. The Absentees did not appear to make any allowances, even when it was known that individual teachers (frequently a form teacher) had bent over backwards to help or be kind to them. Most teachers were seen, therefore, as representatives of unfavoured and rejected institutions whose job was to promote learning and good attendance, two processes which the Absentees had already disregarded. Hence, teachers (and other professionals) have to be prepared for the possibility that their most skilful attempts at intervention will be rejected by absentees without good reason, perhaps even when some 'progress' has been made. Teachers should not be too disappointed if and when this does happen and certainly they should not take it personally. From the opposite perspective, and despite all the mitigating circumstances, the findings obtained from the grids are a condemnation of the pastoral work of teachers. Clearly, very few teachers enamoured themselves to the Absentees, or eased their problems in school. There can be little wonder, therefore, that a high proportion of absentees associate teachers with failure and conflict. In their eyes, this is justified.

8

Institutional Aspects of Non-attendance

The Search for Institutional Measures

There has been an imbalance in work undertaken into the various aspects of school absenteeism and truancy. Far more investigations have been carried out into the social and psychological than the institutional factors associated with non-attendance (Reid and Kendall, 1982). There are several reasons for this.

First, most of the research conducted before the mid-seventies strongly emphasised the close link which exists between truancy and absenteeism, home backgrounds, familial features, poverty, poor housing and social disadvantage (see Chapters 5 and 6).

Second, influential work conducted in the United States purported to show that individual schools had only slight effects upon their pupils when compared with the greater effects of social class (Jencks *et al.*, 1972; Bowles and Gintis, 1976). It is known that these pioneer studies were heavily laden with familial and social rather than educational variables. Their findings therefore merely reflected the fact that those features of schools that do have an impact upon the pupils had not been identified or sufficiently taken into consideration. Thus, the lack of a relationship between identifiable school attributes and pupil outcomes could not have been achieved (Reynolds *et al.*, 1980).

Third, early studies in Britain into the relationship between schools and their effects upon pupils met with considerable opposition because they were seen as posing ideological and political as well as 'practical' threats to schools. For instance, potentially important work by Michael Power and his colleagues (1967, 1972) into the different effects schools have in generating a variety of levels of delinquency was stopped by the Inner London Education Authority and the National Union of Teachers before meaningful results could be obtained. Fortunately, the decision to publish the results of school reports based on visits undertaken by HM Inspectors may counteract this tendency. For instance, several HMI reports have already been strongly critical (HMI, 1982) of schools' attendance rates.

Nevertheless, researchers who attempt to undertake school-based studies into the institutional factors involved in truancy and school absenteeism will continue to walk a professional, as well as methodological, tightrope for some years to come. How researchers tackle these attendant problems will be crucial to the outcome. In particular, researchers are frequently placed in invidious positions when they are given, or obtain, certain kinds of 'confidential' information. For example, in my own study, a fourth year male absentee informed me that he had participated in stealing from and vandalising several primary schools in the area over a two year period without ever having been caught or prosecuted.

Likewise, there is little doubt that many teachers are oblivious of the fact that they, as well as parents, share a major blame for the non-attendance of pupils at school. Moreover, some would rather ignore enquiring too deeply into the reasons why pupils miss school, preferring to leave this matter to heads of year and education welfare officers.

Fourth, the dearth of research into the relationship between schools and absenteeism *per se* has itself handicapped researchers because it has meant that there have been few guiding studies and leads available to assist potential investigators in formulating their research designs and methodologies. Nevertheless, hints could have been obtained from the large number of theoretical and empirical studies which have suggested that the relationship between school policies and social outcomes is too obvious to be ignored (Cohen, 1955; Miller, 1958; Cloward and Ohlin, 1961; Cicourel and Kitsuse, 1963; Mays, 1964; Stinchcombe, 1964; Hargreaves, 1967; Hargreaves *et al.*, 1975; Little, 1977). The notorious William Tyndale enquiry, for example, showed a clear relationship exists between overt bad practice and educational outcomes (Auld, 1976). This enquiry is a classic example of parents, the local education authority and the Department of Education and Science co-operating vigorously to redress the balance of poor school 'management' when the public interest is at stake. Whether substantially unfavourable HMI reports will arouse similar responses in the future must remain an open question. It is likely that this will prove to be another delicate matter because local interests and policies, as well as political and human considerations, can influence subsequent events.

Independent evidence obtained from studies into school differences has reported substantial variations between schools in their rates of delinquency (Power, 1967; Power *et al.*, 1972), child guidance referrals (Gath, 1972) and behavioural problems (Rutter, 1973). Galloway *et al.* (1982) and Grunsell (1980) both found marked differences between schools in their rates of pupil suspension and Galloway's (1980a, 1982) project confirmed that these differences were unrelated to variations in the catchment areas.

Likewise, Bird *et al.* (1980) have reported that schools differ in their use of off-site units for disruptive pupils. This reflects the different practices which exist within institutions for handling difficult pupils. For example, while some schools openly refer pupils at the first sign of disaffection, others refer them for specialist advice and attention as a last resort when everything else has failed (Tattum, 1982).

Such research indicates that internal school policies within individual schools (organisation, ethos and practice) do effect outcomes – favourably and unfavourably. To some extent, therefore, schools are accountable for their actions.

School Differences and Attendance

The acclaimed, but in some ways, controversial school differences studies of David Reynolds (Reynolds, 1976, 1977; Reynolds *et al.*, 1976, 1980; Reynolds and Murgatroyd, 1977; Reynolds and Jones, 1978) and Michael Rutter and his colleagues (1979) have been extensively reported, criticised, summarised and reviewed (Reynolds and Sullivan, 1979; Reynolds and Reid, 1985) by the media and academic press alike, and have stimulated a great deal of popular as well as educational interest. Reynolds investigated nine secondary schools in a homogeneous valley in industrial South Wales and found that their attendance records varied considerably. His work showed that high attendance schools are characterised by small size, lower institutional control, less rigorous enforcement of certain key rules on pupil behaviour, higher co-option of pupils as prefects, and close parent-school relationships. By contrast, high truancy schools seem to be narrowly 'custodial' in orientation, with high levels of control, harsh and strict rule enforcement and a gulf between teachers and pupils and their parents. Reynolds suggests, therefore, that some schools with low rates of truancy and delinquency establish a kind of 'truce' situation whereby some working-class pupils escape punishment for breaking school rules in exchange for co-operation in other aspects of school life. This is tacitly accepted by staff as a means by which they can cope with the existing and disproportionate levels of inequality and social distress and so enables schools to accommodate pupils who otherwise do not share their dominant values.

The work of Reynolds also accords well with the findings of Finlayson and Loughran (1976) which reported that teachers in high delinquency schools are perceived by their pupils as hostile and authoritarian in their classroom dealings. Similar research undertaken in the United States also confirms this view (Rafilides and Hoy, 1971).

Bird *et al.* (1980) report a similar phenomenon in the London schools which they studied but are critical of the practice. They found that it is not unusual in some schools to ignore pupil absence, exclude pupils from lessons and barter for good behaviour which, in effect, allows individual pupils to opt out of the mainstream and follow personalised programmes.

Another superficial trend in some schools is to allow disaffected pupils to be legally off the school premises and so avoid confrontation situations as often as possible. Specifically, the increase in activities like traffic and population 'surveys', *ad hoc* community schemes and industrial visits in such lessons as social studies and humanities bears partial testimony to this trend.

In my own research, I found that many of the 'good attenders' in the same forms as the Persistent Absentees were at least, or even more, alienated from their school on some issues than the poor attenders. Indeed, my subjective impression is that a number of alienated pupils who are not absentees attend school for compensatory social (peer group friendships, mutual activity) rather than good educational reasons.

The research of Rutter and his colleagues (1979) has confirmed the importance of a good school ethos or climate in achieving favourable school outcomes. This team found that the most successful schools encourage a prompt start to lessons, place a strong emphasis on academic progress and attainment, have generally low levels of punishment, recognise positively pupils' achievements within schools, have well cared for buildings and foster good teacher–pupil relationships to such an extent that students feel they can approach staff to help them with their personal problems. This latter point is important because I (Reid, 1982e, 1983c) found that persistent absentees are less likely to approach school staff with their problems than good attenders.

Finally, the HMI report (1977) on ten secondary schools highlights and reinforces similar results to those of the Rutter team. This report suggests that good schools are characterised by careful preparation of lessons, variety of approach, regular and constructive correction of pupils' work and consistent encouragement.

The findings of Reynolds, Rutter *et al.* and HM Inspectorate accord well with one another; this is particularly interesting given that Rutter's and Reynolds' work were undertaken in such dissimilar regions as a South Wales mining valley and Inner London. The findings obtained from both studies appear to suggest that pupils do better in schools which manifest old-fashioned rather than *laissez-faire* virtues. It seems that pupils generally like to be kept busy, have corporate spirit fostered and react favourably to good professional practice. Schools and teachers who 'opt out' of this approach tend to lose far more than they gain. Nevertheless, much more research, in particular, pioneer, in-depth, school-based qualitative studies, is needed before definitive conclusions can be reached on the relationship between institutional policy and school outcomes.

The fact that particular school policies can and do affect individual pupils and their attendance habits as well as school outcomes will not surprise many teachers. For instance, by the late sixties Clegg and Megson (1968) reported that a poor school ethos undermines pupils' progress. At the time, they were concerned with the way in which school practices divided the slower pupils from the quick, the bright from the less able, as these measures seemed to reinforce and exacerbate the inherent disadvantages of the weaker children. Whether subsequent groupings – such as mixed ability teaching – have eased these problems is a complex and emotive issue about which many teachers have their own opinions!

Implications for Practitioners

Large and consistent variations in the levels of truancy and school attendance cannot be solely explained by such factors as geographical location and pupils' social backgrounds. Two schools located in similar parts of a town can have vastly differing rates of attendance. It seems, therefore, that attendance rates are at least partially influenced by what takes place within school time. Research into school differences suggests that schools need to look very closely at their own policies and relate them to such issues as non-attendance, delinquency, vandalism, conflict, disruption and alienation.

Murgatroyd (1974, 1976, 1977) has presented evidence which should alarm many schools and in particular the pastoral care staff. He shows that the claims of some schools to have promoted pastoral care and counselling services which endeavour to achieve the humanistic goals of self-actualisation, personal development and the acquisition of coping strategies are far from accurate and even exaggerated. His work suggests staff should constantly review the effectiveness of the pastoral work in which they are involved. Without such evaluation, pastoral work in schools will continue to be undertaken more as an act of faith than as having a scientific basis.

As mentioned earlier, there is a substantial body of opinion throughout education which maintains that many secondary schools only cater well for the very bright and least able child. The large majority in the middle bands tend to receive much less and less good attention for a whole variety of reasons. It may be that if real progress is to be made in this complex area British researchers will need to take a lead from their counterparts in the United States by measuring such difficult concepts as school ethos (Reynolds and Reid, 1985).

Notwithstanding potential methodological problems, the time has surely come for teachers to act as researchers within their own schools in order to uncover original data on the real outcomes of schooling for less able and disadvantaged pupils (such as truants and absentees) as well as high achievers (Reynolds and Reid, 1985). The teacher-as-researcher concept (Stenhouse, 1975; Pring, 1978; Hopkins, 1982) potentially offers a most valuable medium for promoting relatively cheap and effective projects which may help to stimulate and promote better and more effective in-service work and personal development and contribute to the discipline of education (Hopkins and Reid, 1985). Without this initiative, it could well be that the differences between and within schools will never be properly explained and understood, since every school is unique.

9

Educational Facets

The State of the Art

The large-scale school differences studies reported in Chapter 8 have provided a much needed boost to the search for evidence on the relationship between schooling and non-attendance. However, while these projects have generated much interesting data, they have fallen some way short of supplying crucial information on the quality of the interaction between teachers and absentees.

Two dichotomous attitudes seem to be prevalent among educationists about the part which schools play in preventing or encouraging absenteeism. The first theory was offered by Boyson (1974) who argued that truancy is increasing as a result of changing and deteriorating educational methods and standards. Boyson expressed what is, after all, a widespread, if largely unsubstantiated, belief, that alienation, disaffection and absenteeism (as described in the Black Papers) have all increased since the introduction of comprehensive education (see Chapter 2, page 16).

Conversely, Reynolds *et al*. (1976) have consistently argued on the basis of their own findings the opposite point of view. They contend that some aspects of traditional teaching and schooling, with its insistence on the maintenance of certain rules at all costs and the use of corporal punishment, lead to conflict between teachers and pupils with the result that schools suffer from such unpleasant manifestations as internal vandalism and external truancy and delinquency.

Both these points of view have their merits. Indeed, they may not even be mutually exclusive. As every school has different emphases and policies, the truth probably lies mid-way between the two extremes dependent upon such facets as teachers' abilities, the effectiveness of the headteacher and the school's pastoral care teams, as well as parent–school relationships.

Pupils' Perceptions

Surprisingly little research into absenteeism and truancy has relied upon pupils' own perceptions. One reason for this may have been the advice given by such experts as Stott (1966) and Tyerman (1968) who felt that investigating truants' perceptions of their schools was likely to prove fruitless, possibly because they were dubious about the amount of credibility which could be given to these kinds of data.

Based on experiences during my own fieldwork, I can confirm that there are *some* grounds for Stott's and Tyerman's fears. Nevertheless, the opposite point of view is equally tenable. When a researcher listens to one, two or even several non-attenders being critical about a school's ethos, the teachers and the curriculum, then he or she is right to be justifiably cautious. After I had listened to 128 Persistent Absentees individually giving versions of the same theme, I began to feel inclined to believe that their views had some merit. Generally speaking, it is a fact that a question to a persistent absentee about his or her non-attendance is likely to be followed by an answer about one or other aspect of school life (see Chapter 10).

My own social anthropological approach and the work of previous researchers have suggested that factors within schools which unwittingly 'contribute' to pupils' non-attendance include a dislike of school, all kinds of school transfers, the curriculum and examinations, bullying and allied traits, 'difficult' peer group relationships, disruptive behaviour, school rules, punishment, unfavourable relationships with teachers, the teaching ability of staff, unsatisfactory timetables and the reactions of peers and teachers when absentees return to school after a short or long absence.

Dislike of School

Mitchell and Shepherd (1967) analysed data obtained from 6000 primary and secondary children attending school in Buckinghamshire in the days of selection. They found that a dislike (as opposed to a fear) of school was strongly associated with poor attainment and signs of anxiety at home. Their work suggests that certain pupils react against their schools by staying away once they are old enough to make these decisions and have weighed up the consequences.

To some extent, the work of Mitchell and Shepherd is confirmed by Eaton and Houghton's (1974) Northern Ireland study. The latter researchers compared and contrasted the attitudes and expectations of persistent school absentees with good attenders in grammar schools in the Province. They concluded that school absenteeism does appear to be linked with adolescents' levels of satisfaction about their schools. Clearly, therefore, pupils who enjoy their schooling are less likely deliberately to miss school.

School Transfers

I (1983b) found that approximately one in six of my sample of Persistent Absentees claimed that they first decided to miss school because of a school transfer of one kind or another and approximately half of these pupils gave this as a reason for continuing to miss school. Some of the Absentees' responses suggested that they felt less attached to their secondary than to their primary schools. They also disliked the internal organisation within comprehensive schools, such as moving classrooms and changing teachers for every lesson.

One pupil whose change of school was precipitated by his mother's move from the north to the south of the city, specifically stated that while he liked his former school he disliked his new school intensely, especially the staff. He bitterly regretted his change of address and on more than one occasion 'mitched' to be with his old friends in his former school. However, instances were also found of pupils' behaviour and attendance being improved after transfers between schools took place for socio-medical and other reasons although, of course, these pupils lay outside the scope of the three samples in my study (see Introduction, page 2).

The Curriculum and Absenteeism

There have been few studies relating the curriculum to non-attendance. This is a serious and surprising omission because it is apparent that some pupils deliberately miss school in order to avoid unpopular lessons (Sullivan and Riches, 1976; ILEA, 1981).

One of the reasons why so little research has been undertaken in this complex and important area may be that it is very difficult to 'apply' and generalise findings from individual schools across the board. Specifically, research of this kind tends to require qualitative rather than quantitative approaches.

Nevertheless, I (1983a) contrived to group the Absentees' responses on various aspects of their school curriculum into meaningful categories (arts, sciences, technical and non-academic subjects) in order to glean some meaningful clues. From these data, the following key facts emerged:

1   The Absentees appeared to favour a 'traditional' curriculum based on maths, English, technical and vocational subjects. In particular, they specifically stated that they would have appreciated more individual help with the basics such as reading, writing and arithmetic. It may well be that a lot of pupils begin to miss school when they fall behind or start to feel uncomfortable in the basics. Many of the Absentees regarded French as being peripheral to their immediate needs and future requirements. Similarly, a higher proportion of male than female Absentees preferred physical education.
2   The Absentees chose a lower ratio of subjects which they enjoyed in school than the two control groups. On average, the Absentees only selected two to three subjects which they enjoyed when in school. By contrast, the pupils in Control Groups 1 and 2 chose four or five subjects respectively.
3   The academic controls tended to be taught by better qualified and

more experienced staff than the absentees and matching controls from the same forms even within the same subject disciplines. If this trend could be substantiated by further research, it may well give a substantial clue as to why some pupils more than others reject schools (see pages 92–3).

4   Certain subjects were universally unpopular with all three groups: for example, religious education. This subject is cited because the headteachers in the two schools considered that they were extremely fortunate with the ability of their existing religious education teachers. Therefore, the results were probably as much influenced by the nature and content of the subject as the teaching aspects.

Bird *et al.* (1980) found that certain pupils form adverse opinions of their curriculum if they perceive it as being irrelevant, if they are unable to relate to its academic slant, if they cannot meet the demands it makes, and if the content or teaching style or teaching input leaves them feeling failures (see also Tattum, 1982). Certainly, my own enquiry showed that there is a marked decline in the progress of non-attenders prior to and following their absences as measured by comments and grades on their school reports/files. Moreover, several researchers including York *et al.* (1972), Varlaam (1974), Fogelman (1978), Anderson (1980), Buist (1980), Lawrence *et al.* (1981) and Galloway *et al.* (1982) have variously reported that disruptive and absentee children frequently under-achieve, are backward at school and experience difficulties in understanding and learning what they are taught. Hence, they tend to manifest conduct disorders in order to obviate their failure.

Fogelman (1976) examined data obtained from the National Child Development study and found a relationship between attendance and attainment which was reduced, but remained statistically significant, even after allowing for related social factors such as class. By contrast, he reported little correlation between attainment at the age of 16 and attendance rates in the primary school.

5   The evidence from these data clearly suggested that absentees are more apathetic in lessons than their classmates. This raises an interesting question. Is learning *per se* reduced in importance once pupils start to miss school or is it one of the prices these pupils have to pay for their non-attendance?

The Curriculum and Examinations

Many truants and absentees tend to come from the lower bands of secondary schools. Although pupils may not experience much external assessment within school until the fifth year, it is obvious that they soon perceive messages about their real academic ability in a variety of ways – the success of more able pupils, teachers' comments, intuition, inability to read or follow certain materials or books, as well as the degree and type of help which they receive in class.

Many teachers believe that as soon as pupils are classified as non-examinees, they tend to lower their academic ceilings and become increasingly disaffected within school. For this reason, it is widely thought that all pupils should leave school with some form of school-leaving certificate. The opposite is sometimes held to be true. Forcing less able pupils to sit internal and external examinations is believed by some to be a waste of time for all concerned in the enterprise. On a more delicate note, there is a widespread belief that some teachers, even those whose records with high ability bands of pupils are extremely good, try less hard with lower ability forms because they are not so highly motivated for this kind of work. So far, however, research has failed to prove this.

Mary

Mary was a bright girl with a measured intelligence quotient of almost 120 at the age of 11. Her conduct, attendance and progress at primary school were described as 'excellent' and following her transfer to secondary school, she was put into an 'A' band. Shortly after arriving at the comprehensive, she began missing school because she did not like her new form and could not relate to the teachers in the school. In the second year, she was demoted to a 'B' band at her own request after gradually falling further and further behind in her work. In the fourth year, she was demoted again to a 'C' band mainly because her attendance was so appalling. The following year she left school without any 'O' level or CSE passes or a school-leaving certificate.

Throughout her interviews she maintained that the main reason for her original non-attendance lay in the way she was taught and the content of her lessons. She complained bitterly about the stupidity of note-taking in every lesson and of the frequent use of 'tests' in class by the teachers. Mary argued that she would never have become an absentee if she hadn't been forced to take certain subjects. In particular, she claimed she intensely disliked swimming and having to stand around getting cold during games lessons.

At no time did the school attempt to pacify Mary's feelings. Instead it insisted that she attend every lesson, or by implication, none at all. Mary chose the latter course and has since bitterly regretted her decision. Last heard of, she had been out of work for over two years and was suffering from depression.

Bullying

I (1983b) found that no fewer than 15 and 19 per cent of my sample respectively claimed that they first missed school and later continued to miss school for reasons associated with bullying in the widest sense of the term. In addition, in one of the two schools (see Introduction, page 2), a certain amount of extortion was evident, especially amongst the black pupils. Although the school was aware of the problem, it was not very successful in eradicating it, probably because of its furtive nature. It is unlikely that the relationship between bullying and persistent absenteeism would be so high in many schools in different parts of Britain. Even in South Wales, such rumblings and undercurrents are unusual. One Absentee, for example, first claimed to 'mitch' school when his football cards were 'stolen' by some of the peers in his class. Another started to miss school when he failed to pay a fine of 2p a day imposed on him by his classmates. This small sum was payable as protection money. If the sum was not paid, the pupil was bullied until such time as the payments started again.

Another facet of the problem, the reported tendency for more boys than girls to be influenced by acts which they described as bullying, is likely to be replicated in future studies. Teachers need to remember that comparatively minor incidents can assume major proportions in the minds of young, largely immature, pupils.

Peer Group Relationships

In an early but important study Croft and Grygier (1956) used a sociometric technique to investigate the interaction between truants and their peers. They found that truants tend to have few friends, but, when they are placed in classes for the backward, they are more likely to be better integrated. It is interesting that delinquents were found to be more outgoing and accepted by their peers than truants.

Some support for the work of Croft and Grygier comes from Tyerman (1968) who described his truant sample as tending to be shy loners. By contrast, Ralphson (1973) looked at the friendship patterns of pupils in his remedial department and found them to be inversely related to the amount of absence.

Mitchell (1972) reported that poor attenders are more often inclined to associate with friends from their own localities who do not go to the same institution than good attenders, who are more frequently to be found in the company of pupils from their own schools.

On the basis of the pupils' own perceptions, I (1984a) ascertained that persistent absentees and academic band pupils tend to have significantly fewer friends in school and in the same forms than good attenders from the same classes. As suggested earlier, it seems that some pupils from deprived home backgrounds and with roughly similar intellectual abilities as absentees attend school for compensatory social reasons. Further sociometric research conducted on a number of different samples of absentees and good attenders is necessary before too many firm conclusions can be reached on this issue. The fundamental importance of peer group unpopularity should never be overlooked, however, as a serious explanation of some, if not much, absenteeism from school.

School Rules and Punishment

All schools have rules of one kind or another; they can generally be sub-divided into two kinds. The first sort – general prescriptive rules – cover such facets as uniform, personal appearance, running in corridors, attending assembly, not smoking and interpersonal behaviour within schools. The second kind are rules in the classroom concerning conduct, talk, movement and work.

This subject was investigated by Hargreaves *et al.* (1975) in one of the most important and useful projects of its kind to be undertaken. They analysed the rules and regulations which operate within classrooms and the ways in which routine deviance is expressed by pupils and imputed by teachers. Their work should be read by all teachers who have an interest in the difficult, slow or disaffected child as it highlights the methods of social typing which arc commonly used by teachers to define pupils as rule breakers and troublemakers. Moreover, it illustrates the kinds of strategies which are frequently utilised by staff to maintain discipline and order in the classroom.

In most comprehensive schools today, pupils have to show considerable levels of sophistication in order to be able to cope with the different levels of behaviour expected of them in their schools and classrooms. For instance, in the first lesson of the day, pupils may be allowed to chat freely amongst themselves, wear coats and eat sweets. In the following class, rigid standards may be enforced to prevent all these forms of behaviour and expression. There is no norm. Teachers set their own standards within classrooms based on creating the kind of atmosphere in which they feel most comfortable. It is not surprising that some pupils are confused by the different standards which are expected of them, although, of course, some are better able to cope with and adapt to these situations than others. Truants and absentees, who attend school irregularly, inevitably find themselves in trouble of one sort or another because of such issues as their non-attendance, attitude, dress, unpunctuality, lack of progress and, in some cases, misconduct (Reynolds, 1975, 1977; Reynolds *et al.*, 1980). I (Reid, 1982a), for example, describe a Persistent Absentee who returned to school after a long absence and was promptly sent home again by a senior member of staff for wearing the wrong colour pullover. In such instances, rule enforcement goes beyond the bounds of logic and common sense.

Some pupils, who feel constantly rejected by the traditional academic and cultural values which schools extol and enforce, are inclined to set up their own counter-school culture. This manifests itself in a variety of ways

(Hargreaves *et al.*, 1975; Willis, 1977; Marsh *et al.*, 1978) and becomes a means for disaffected and deviant pupils to raise their own and their peers' estimations and as a result becomes an alternative source of esteem and status.

Tattum (1982) has argued that disruptive (and by implication non-conformist) behaviour should not be condemned or condoned but used constructively to examine the problematic features (grey areas) of life inside schools. Beresford and Croft (1982) go even further. They suggest that disaffection with school is a common experience in young people and is fostered by the use of antiquated rules and regulations. They argue that major reforms within schools are needed. In particular, they would like to see individualised and constructive responses, rather than rigid penal ones, for non-conformist behaviour. Based on their own experience working with young people in the community, they believe that if such imaginative actions were taken by people in authority, more positive attitudes towards school would be instigated. In turn, they believe this would, amongst other things, ensure better attendance. Whether this argument is correct must for the moment remain an open question given the lack of research and positive leads in this complex field.

Relationships with Teachers

Good pupil–teacher relationships are fundamental if pupils are to enjoy and respond positively to their schooling. A great deal of evidence now exists which shows that many absentees believe they are picked on unfairly, not treated with respect, handled inconsistently and dealt with too harshly (Seabrook, 1974; Sullivan and Riches, 1976; Scottish Education Department, 1977; Buist, 1980; Tattum, 1982).

Control in classrooms is, however, the one issue which teachers and student-teachers (Patrick *et al.*, 1982) believe can make or break them. Teachers unable to cope with difficult classes and/or individual pupils may on occasions find themselves needing to withdraw from the situation (Dunham, 1977). Hence, teachers learn to develop their own form of coping strategies which are aimed at preventing and withstanding challenges to their authority (Hargreaves *et al.*, 1975; Leach, 1977). This is especially true amongst classes which include a large percentage of disillusioned and difficult pupils, often in their final years at school.

Although many teachers manage to cope in these situations, some do not. There are teachers who tend to over-react in circumstances which appear to challenge their authority or when they encounter non-conformist behaviour both in and out of the classroom. Care must be taken over what is said to non-attenders and how sentiments are expressed. Excessive strictness and unjust punishments can provoke hostile reactions and long-term resentment amongst some pupils (Lawrence *et al.*, 1981; Shostak, 1982). Moreover, repeated confrontation situations can lead to excessive teacher stress, thereby creating a vicious circle in which the very outcome the teacher's original action was meant to forestall is aggravated.

I (Reid, 1983b) found that only five and 14 per cent respectively of my sample of Persistent Absentees claimed that they began or continued to miss school because of the staff in their schools. It is very hard, however, to disassociate teacher-instigated reactions from other aspects of school life because staff attitudes and policies impinge on every facet of school life (see Chapter 10, page 98ff.).

In addition, there is virtually no research which relates the ability, qualifications and experience of teachers to absenteeism. It seems highly probable that some absentees resent the fact that the lower ability bands are often taught by the least able, least qualified and least experienced staff. Apart from anything else, this is one way in which 'C' band pupils perceive themselves as receiving different and poorer treatment than their 'A' band peers (Hargreaves, 1967).

Finally, sarcastic and unfavourable comments from teachers and peers alike, as well as the fear of punishment on return to school, are other reasons why some pupils continue to stay away from school once they have taken the initial plunge or graduate to the persistent stage (ILEA, 1981).

Implications for Practitioners

Teachers need to understand the formative and influential role they fulfil with young people. Every word they say and every action they take can affect the way in which pupils think about and act within schools, not least towards the teachers. Words as well as deeds are powerful tools. Teachers often tend to forget that with under-achieving pupils words of praise and encouragement can have more effect than any kind of punishment.

The same is true of the written word. In my own enquiry, for example, a form teacher wrote the following on an internal school report: '. . . it is no wonder she misses so much school coming from a family like that and after her sister caused the school so much trouble. She's doing everyone a favour by staying away. I only wish we could find a way of removing her for good.' On another school report, a subject teacher wrote of a persistent absentee: '. . . makes brilliant progress when in class – which is never'.

Similarly, much more thought is needed on the way pupils' options and compulsory subjects are selected. This is especially true in the third year of many secondary schools because pupils soon realise when they are being 'cast asunder' by being placed in non-examination sets. No doubt, this is one of the reasons why absenteeism significantly increases at this stage (see Chapters 2, page 14ff., and 4, page 44ff). In what ways senior teachers can take pupils' choices and parental wishes into sufficient account when they have to find ways and means of ensuring viable groups is always a vexed and thorny issue. It may well be that too many at-risk pupils are put into situations where insufficient endeavour is expected of them and where there are no tangible goals for hard work and enterprise, irrespective of ability.

Likewise, pupils' timetables are not always as carefully thought out as they should be. For instance, on one school day some pupils may get six academic lessons in succession, maths, English, history, geography, religious education and science. On another, the same pupils may get several 'non-academic' classes, home economics, woodwork, rural studies, physical education, games and personal development. This extreme situation is unlikely but illustrates the point, as the tendency for some pupils to develop specific day and/or lesson absence is well known.

There is a general tendency in some teaching situations for staff to under-estimate the difficulties which pupils may have in responding to or understanding instructions. An inability to undertake set tasks well can lead some pupils to develop an acute sense of failure and inferiority. Not all teachers talk as clearly and precisely as they might, nor give sufficient individual time for slow workers or less able pupils. Often they are unable to do so because of the size of the class, demands of the syllabus, the need to maintain order and, in mixed ability situations, the requirements of the most able and/or the majority. Nevertheless, some teachers may not always expect or foster high enough standards of work from the less able and/or difficult pupils. The maintenance of high standards and strong motivation with lower ability bands is a serious problem.

Too few teachers tend to acknowledge the crucial part which schools play in the prevention of truancy. Murgatroyd (1974), for example, reported that only seven per cent of teachers holding pastoral posts accepted that some of the responsibility for the behaviour of truants rested with their schools. He further suggested that the colleagues of these teachers would regard any acceptance of truants' explanations for their behaviour as signs of weakness in the post-holder. Throughout the teaching profession, the acceptance of pupil explanations, without clear proof, is often regarded as weakening the authority of the school to decide what is and what is not in the pupils' best interests.

In a later study, Murgatroyd (1977) investigated the perceptions of 424 pupils from one comprehensive school in South Wales of their school counsellors. He found that the pupils ranked the three following activities as the most important functions of the counsellors: checking attendance registers; being responsible for lost property; and reporting truants to the education welfare officer. Although the counsellors in the schools saw themselves as caring people, they were largely perceived as 'deputies' by the pupils who expected them to perform similar functions as administrative middle management in schools.

Another issue needs to be raised, that of teacher absence. In Britain, there has been little research undertaken into this delicate subject, probably because of the threatening and 'political' implications of the work. No such sanctity has been observed in the United States (Board of Education, 1960; Gibson, 1964). Even in Britain, however, it has long been popular 'gossip' in certain staff-rooms that certain teachers appear to be absent on some days more regularly than on others – usually when they have 4X or 5K. Some educationists believe that teacher absenteeism has increased since the raising of the school-leaving age, the change-over to comprehensive education, the tendency for the size of schools to increase in the seventies and unfavourable and changing school climates. It seems that certain teachers are just as errant as some pupils.

10

Inside the Schools

This chapter concentrates on some of the findings of my own in-depth, pioneer study into persistent school absenteeism in two large comprehensive schools in industrial South Wales using a social anthropological approach (Mead, 1973; Stubbs and Delamont, 1976). These are not reported elsewhere in the book. The data were obtained from talking to and interviewing 128 Persistent School Absentees and two control groups from the third, fourth and fifth years throughout one academic year. Some of these pupils were formally interviewed as many as 16 times, and were also observed on other informal occasions. In a few cases, home visits were made towards the end of the fieldwork in order to complete the profiles of each pupil.

The two schools had similar catchment area difficulties and overt academic policies which were only partially succeeding. The size, buildings and internal organisation within the two schools were very different. Both schools had poor attendance records which they were treating in much the same way – and not succeeding very well. Finally, the 'climates' of the two schools could not have been more different. The staff in School A, for all their immense problems, always appeared convivial, helpful and cheerful. Conversely, School B gave the impression of being embattled, miserable and generally unhappy about the over rigorous disciplinary attitude of the senior staff towards themselves and the children – a situation which many of the teachers believed contributed to the non-attendance habits of the pupils.

The Social Anthropological Approach

The social anthropological approach is being used increasingly in educational research. The methodology is derived from anthropology which is concerned with biological evolution of human beings and classification of living races (Good and Brophy, 1978). Researchers following a social anthropological approach tend to immerse themselves in the group they are studying and talk freely with respondents using participant observation methods, conducting interviews and keeping field notes, which are both systematic and open ended. Such researchers make no attempt to manipulate, control or eliminate variables. Instead the breadth of the enquiry is reduced gradually in order to focus on the emerging issues. It was this formula that I adopted, and in this way I obtained information from pupils, teachers, senior staff, secretaries, social workers, education welfare officers, a youth officer, school reports, records, case reports and a range of other papers and school documents, including registers.

The selection of the Persistent Absentees and two control groups was a vital preliminary process and was made after consultation with senior staff, form teachers and education welfare officers as appropriate, in order to comply with the research design and operational definition (see Chapter 1, pages 6–7). Each Absentee was matched by age and sex with two controls – one from the same form and one from an academic band. The two control groups were comprised of pupils with as exemplary attendance histories as possible.

After selecting the Persistent Absentees and two control groups, there followed an initial exploratory interview with each individual. Only very general introductory information was recorded: name, form, number of years in the school, age and willingness to participate in the study.

From the second interview onwards, an attempt was made to develop the personal biographies of the Persistent Absentees. Thereafter, schedules were devised for seeing the pupils. This process incorporated the use of special forms (approved by the school) which were placed in registers before the start of each day and countersigned by senior staff. These enabled the control group pupils to be withdrawn from non-academic classes and the Absentees from any classes. Owing to the Absentees' non-attendance, the weather and demands of the curriculum, a flexible system was adopted whereby some pupils could be seen for a long session (up to half a day at a time in exceptional cases), whilst others were interviewed on several shorter occasions. Gradually, therefore, a relationship developed between the pupils and myself.

Some interviews were straightforward, others demanded considerably more skill and patience. For instance, the early interviews with one fourth year girl were largely a waste of time because she consistently lied. Later, as her confidence grew, she became more co-operative to the extent that she began to make morning coffee for me whenever she was in school.

It was considered essential that I was not seen by the pupils as an extension of the school establishment. For this reason the location of the interviews was important. Hence, the interviews were conducted in one school in the Youth Centre which was ideal.

As time passed, a substantial amount of data was accumulated on each pupil. An interesting but unusual phenomenon took place in a few instances; this manifested itself in three ways. Firstly, certain Absentees from School A were found to visit (rather than attend) the school only on those days when they were due to see me even though they were marked absent in the register. On many occasions, these pupils completed their interviews, turned round and walked straight out of the school. Secondly, the loyalty to the project of both the poor and good attenders was amazing. Towards the end of the year (when much data needed to be gathered on certain pupils) letters requesting help were sent to the pupils' home addresses. These usually sufficed. Thirdly, by the end of the project, a few Absentees voluntarily acted as 'bookies runners' by taking the appropriate forms to their counterparts. This process also engendered confidence and fostered co-operation from the Persistent Absentees.

The good relationship which gradually built up between the pupils and myself considerably eased the transition from the social anthropological to the quantitative approaches which are reported elsewhere in the book. These data were all completed in one-to-one or small group situations as circumstances and the requirements of the instruments permitted.

a   The Pupils' Perceptions

1   School Likes and Dislikes

The views of the three groups were sought on their reasons for enjoying or disliking school. The findings showed that more than twice as many of the Control Group 2 pupils had social reasons ('seeing my friends in school', 'playing in the school teams'); academic reasons ('the learning of different languages', 'learning about new things', 'reading', 'taking tests', 'the stimulating lessons'), and non-academic reasons ('looking after the play group on Wednesday afternoons') for enjoying school when compared with the Absentees and Control Group 1 pupils. Thirty-eight per cent of the Absentees and 42 per cent of the Control Group 1 pupils stated that they enjoyed nothing about school. By contrast, this only applied to four per cent of the academic Controls. These data highlight the extent to which schools are more rewarding places for able than for less able pupils irrespective of attendance.

The Absentees gave a total of 284 reasons for disliking school compared with 182 and 85 for the two control groups respectively. At least twice as many Absentees and Control Group 1 pupils as Control Group 2 pupils claimed they disliked school for teaching/teacher, rules and regulations, curriculum and disciplinary reasons. Almost half the Control Group 2 pupils categorically stated that they had no serious complaints against their schools; the same was true for only a handful of pupils in the other two Groups.

From the interviews, it was apparent that the whole tenor and tone of the pupils' grievances differed from group to group. The Absentees and Control Group 1 pupils made repeated complaints about their schools' policies and general treatment and attitudes towards them, and were disenchanted by the teachers and their teaching styles and the schools' curricula. Quite naturally the Control Group 2 pupils also complained about their schooling, but less vociferously. The nature of their grievances, however, differed quite markedly. Many of these pupils were more concerned, for example, about the volume of work given to them by particular teachers and the lack of science lessons than about 'atmospheric' factors.

2 Criticism of Teachers

Many Absentees and Control Group 1 pupils were repeatedly critical of the attitudes of certain senior teaching staff who they considered to be too harsh and lacking in understanding about their problems. But they were equally scathing of weak teachers. One male Absentee said:

'There is no point in me going to school anyway as we never learn anything. All everyone does is fool around every lesson. One of the teachers is even scared of us. He promises not to give us homework so long as we behave. . . . We've never learnt anything in any of his lessons since we've been here. . . . Some of the others think it's great. I don't. . . . I wanted to learn . . . Now I just think, what's the point?'

Another Absentee remarked: '. . . the teachers are all the same here. They don't care about anybody but themselves. One of them does nothing but complain to us about his salary.'

A member of Control Group 1 asked: '. . . who'd be a teacher anyway? All they get is trouble every day of their lives. And some of them deserve all they get.'

3 School Change

When asked what improvements they would like to see made in their schools, the responses from the pupils were particularly revealing. Almost half of the Absentees, compared with approximately one fifth of the Control Group 1 pupils and a small minority of those in the academic bands, wanted to see better teaching.

Around three times as many Absentees as Control Group 2 pupils wished to see changes in the school rules: to stop, for example, school uniforms being compulsory. A minority, but more Control Group 2 than Absentee and Control Group 1 pupils, wanted changes introduced in the curriculum. Social and administrative aspects of schooling generally received fewer mentions by pupils in all three Groups than teaching, curriculum and rules. Approximately one in three of the academic controls compared with a very small minority of pupils in each of the other two groups could not think of any improvements which their schools could make. Presumably, this was a measure of their satisfaction.

Conversely, around a third of the Absentees and Control Group 1 pupils expressed their dissatisfaction with their schools but were unable to be specific about any changes they would like to see made in the structure and process of their education. This finding may be related to the low ability of some of the pupils in these two groups. Alternatively, the Absentees' responses may have been indicative of the fact that nothing would have made them return permanently to their schools. Certainly some of them were not slow to make this point!

Most remarkably, almost four times as many Control Group 2 pupils as Absentees and twice as many Control Group 2 as Control Group 1 pupils wanted to see disciplinary changes in the schools. Why? A probable explanation is that the academic band pupils rejected the ethos and confrontation nature of life within the lower bands. Some of them were sensitive to the fact that while they conformed to the rules and regulations of their institutions, their less academic peers tended to deviate from these norms. Consequently, from the Control Group 2 pupils' points of view, there were two sets of standards at work in the schools, one for them and one which applied to the rest. During the interviews, some of the academic good attenders bitterly resented the fact that in their opinion non-attenders appeared repeatedly to get away with 'murder', especially when even slight lateness from them might result in severe reprimands.

Some of the Absentees' responses on this issue of school change are worth recording as they provide an interesting insight into the plight of modern schooling from their point of view: 'more help with reading and writing', 'more of your own friends in your forms', 'more facilities at breaks and lunchtimes', 'more careers help', 'more prevention of bullying', 'allow us to attend smaller schools', 'let us leave at 15 with our parents' consent', 'allow the pupils to choose their own timetables', 'less corporal punishment', 'free school meals for everyone', 'stop compulsory swimming', 'more school trips', 'better discipline in the school', 'more social workers in the school', 'allow everyone to take CSE who wants to', 'less colour prejudice in the school', 'give us harder work', 'make the teacher move class every lesson and not the pupils', 'stop the stealing in the school' and 'allow me to come and go from school as I like'.

Some of the more interesting ideas from the two control groups included 'ban all smoking', 'clean and tidy up the school more', 'stop the bus problems on the way to school', 'have a common room for all pupils over 14', 'provide us with a covered area for wet days', 'make all games lessons optional', 'stop assemblies', 'have a shorter registration period', 'pay school children attendance money by age', 'have Wednesday afternoons free', 'let the "C" streams have more success in their books instead of always getting low marks', 'suspend teachers who don't teach us', 'put disruptive pupils into special units away from the school', 'more revision periods before exams', 'more pupil responsibility once you're in the fifth form', 'more individual pupil attention', 'more young teachers', 'give us chairs to sit on in assembly', and 'allow us a school union'.

These responses highlight the lack of unanimity between the pupils' views. Indeed, some of the responses from the pupils were so individualised that they did not fit into any convenient categories. Yet again, the answers aptly illustrate the uniqueness of each pupil's perceptions and, therefore, the corresponding need to use personalised approaches with non-conformist pupils like absentees; blanket approaches are just not likely to work.

b Combating Non-attendance

Given the singular lack of success of existing institutional schemes to persuade persistent absentees to return to school, it was decided to ask the pupils in all three groups for their views on the best way to re-integrate non-attenders into the fold. It is interesting that there was a degree of uniformity between the opinions of the two control groups on this measure but considerable disparity between their views and those of the Absentees.

One quarter of the Absentees (25.7 per cent) took the view that no form of retribution or school change would or could make them become good attenders again. The largest proportion of Absentees (31.3 per cent) thought that all punishment schemes should be restricted to operating solely within the schools. A minority thought that corporal punishment (22 per cent), parent-instigated schemes (such as being kept in at night and/or the withdrawal of pocket money, 13 per cent), and court or other forms of social action (for example, compulsory involvement in community schemes, 8 per cent) would be the only basis for making them return to school. The variation between the Absentees' responses suggests that collectively they themselves are no nearer finding a viable solution than present educational administrators, education welfare officers, the courts and social service departments. Some caution should be applied to these data. First, all the Absentees gave their responses after they had reached the chronic stage. Second, many of them specifically stated that if appropriate remedies had been implemented earlier in their educational histories, then their non-attendance would not have graduated to its present level. Examples of remedies cited by the Absentees included changes of form and form teachers, subject options and timetables, provision of a school uniform, prevention from being bullied, and more home help being given to parents. To be realistic, some of these demands are hardly excessive and may have had a sound basis. The pupils' answers again show the inflexibility of schools and how few pastoral staff take the individual needs of deviant pupils into account. Sometimes, one wonders just how often teachers actually talk and *listen* to absentees and truants. In a sense, the Absentees' responses are indicative of what poor early detection schemes (which currently bedevil work with non-attenders) lead to in the long run. Sometimes, small changes, subtly and speedily implemented at the right time, forestall and prevent some absenteeism. Similarly enlightened approaches might enable some non-attenders to return to their schools without the fear of retribution or loss of face. Surely no great sacrifices are made by schools in acquiescing to such minor requests as a change of form if these subsequently enable previously non-conformist pupils to re-integrate into school life. After all, accommodating pupils' wishes is one way of making them realise that their school cares about them.

Not surprisingly, both the control groups were more in favour of strict action being taken for prolonged school absence than the Absentees themselves. The former thought that lenient action was a waste of time. Schemes which affected parents as well as pupils were considered by the good attenders to be potentially the most effective and were probably secretly feared by the Absentees themselves. Large proportions of the control pupils thought that persistent absenteeism should be punished more heavily by the courts (fining the parents) and through the use of corporal punishment.

Some of the more 'constructive' responses made by the control pupils included: 'do nothing as they are punishing themselves by not learning', 'try a change of form or teachers', 'call their names out in assembly', 'make them work on Saturday afternoons', 'two warnings and then give the parents a fine of at least fifty pounds', 'send them to special schools for truants', 'make more haphazard school checks', 'allow them to be taught by one teacher all day who would collect them and take them home by bus', 'give them extra school duties like the painting of corridors or the cleaning of the toilets', and 'send a social worker to their homes'.

c Help with Problems

Throughout the fieldwork, I gained a strong impression that the pastoral systems in the two schools were hopelessly inadequate and entirely punitive – even harsh. Certainly, my personal observations led me to believe that there was very little sympathy or empathy about when some staff in both schools dealt with the Absentees.

I attempted to ascertain what action the pupils would take if they had a worrying problem in school. In order to obtain these data, I gave three examples to the pupils as the basis for their responses. These were:

– Your mother is very ill and you are concerned about her health.
– A boy has just hit you in the playground for no reason and hurt you.
– You were shouted at in class and put in detention by a teacher for something you did not do.

I then asked the pupils the following question: 'If you were in any, or all, of the three situations written on the card, who would you go and see to discuss your problems in or out of school?' A majority of the Absentees (53 per cent) firmly stated that they would not discuss their problems with anyone. This may have been because they had no confidence in anyone's ability to help them or because they were used to keeping their worries to themselves.

The remainder said they would seek out a teacher (18 per cent), parent (14 per cent), friend (7 per cent), or another source (7 per cent). Significantly, 70 per cent and 54 per cent of the Control Group 2 and 1 pupils respectively stated that they would have sought the help of either a teacher or one or both parents. There is no doubt that these data tend to highlight the poorer personal relationships which exist between many Persistent Absentees and their parents and teachers as compared with good attenders. This is a pathetic situation as absentees and truants are the very people who tend to need help most, indeed, the very pupils for whom pastoral care teams and counsellors were first introduced into schools.

d Pupil Workloads

Another stark reminder of the differences which exist between 'A' and 'C' bands was noted when investigating the pupils' workloads. For example, 55 per cent of the Absentees and Control Group 1 pupils claimed never to have been given any homework in the preceding 12 months. By contrast, all the Control Group 2 pupils were given regular homework. Moreover, over half of these pupils (52 per cent) thought the amount given to them was excessive. Evidence obtained from the interviews suggested that some of the Absentees and Control Group 1 pupils bitterly resented being treated differently from their abler peers on this issue.

Far more of the Control Group 1 than Group 2 and Absentee pupils thought that their general workloads in class were either too heavy or too light. As the Absentees were rarely in school and the needs of the academic pupils were different from the Control Group 1 pupils, no great significance should be attached to this result. Nevertheless, it may be a further pointer that pupil expectation levels are generally lower in 'B' and 'C' bands than 'A' bands.

e Good Teaching

Teachers emerged as crucial factors in the cognitive processes of the Absentees. It is probably significant that a question on school should be followed by an answer about the teachers. Presumably these two aspects are synonymous in the minds of many of absentees. While most of the Absentees (78 per cent) and Control Group 1 (91 per cent) pupils held unfavourable or indifferent opinions of their teachers, the reverse was true for almost half the academic Controls (48 per cent).

Owing to the nature of the pupils' responses, I decided to investigate further the qualities which they looked for in good teachers, despite the criticisms often made of this approach. In this respect, some interesting differences emerged between the three groups. A majority of the Absentees (53 per cent) made comments which suggested that they laid considerable importance on the very process of teaching and classroom management – the role aspects ('help me with my reading and writing', 'keep the others quiet so I can learn', 'allow us to use books like the other kids'). The remainder made comments which reinforced the fundamental importance of teachers' temperaments and personalities (20 per cent), their academic expertise (20 per cent) and administrative abilities (6 per cent). By contrast, the Control Group 1 pupils ranked academic qualities in first place (50 per cent), followed by role (31 per cent), personality (11 per cent) and administration (9 per cent). The Control Group 2 pupils rated personality first (44 per cent), academic ability second (37 per cent), role aspects third (16 per cent), and administrative qualities fourth (2 per cent).

It may seem strange at first glance that the bright pupils placed personality first whilst Control Group 1 pupils thought academic ability most important. Perhaps there is more logic to these responses than is immediately apparent. Many bright pupils find the academic content and presentation of their lessons too 'dry'. Conversely, many 'B' and 'C' band pupils may not think that the academic content of their lessons is sufficiently demanding. If this is the case, this may tell us a great deal about teachers and their teaching approaches and could partially explain a great deal of pupils' current dissatisfaction in schools. Here is another fruitful area for researchers to investigate.

The five most sought after teaching qualities to emerge from the combination of the pupils' responses were: the ability to be strict but fair; the ability to give individual attention to pupils; the ability to assist pupils with their personal problems and/or needs; temperamental aspects such as 'being patient and understanding' and 'having a sense of humour'; the ability to give remedial attention to pupils with these needs.

All these data suggest that pupils in the three groups respected those teachers who were highly motivated, showed a sense of purpose and charismatic leadership qualities and were able to liaise with and control classes. Staff in schools need to remember that good teacher–pupil rapport is established, even with the most difficult classes, as a result of hard work rather than of *laissez-faire* attitudes.

f Home Problems

The home and social disadvantages of absentees and truants were outlined in Chapter 5. Like previous studies undertaken upon truants and absentees, my own sample of Persistent Absentees came from significantly lower social class origins than the good attenders and were more used to familial distress (parental divorce, separations, large households, poor housing, free school meals, paternal/maternal unemployment).

However, despite these findings, a majority (54 per cent) of the Absentees described their relationships with their parents as being fairly good or good. Fifteen per cent stated that their relationships were better with one parent than the other, while the remainder (31 per cent) described their relationships with their parents in such terms as 'poor', 'awful' and 'not very good'. These findings, of course, should not be taken out of context as many of these Absentees were experiencing the trauma of adolescence, being 'adults' with children's features. By contrast, over 90 per cent of both control groups described their relationship with their parents as being good or fairly good.

Some of the Absentees' perceptions of their 'home problems' at the time of the study are quite revealing as they show a wide range and type of familial distress. Incidently, these data were gathered towards the end of the fieldwork once the Absentees were comparatively well known to me.

For example, some of their responses included the following verbatim statements: 'all we ever do is argue at home', 'everything has got worse since my father died', 'being poor', 'shortage of space at home', 'my parents' divorce', 'my mother's bad health', 'my father being disabled', 'being unhappy at home', 'the health of my granny', 'having to share a bed with my two sisters', 'my parents being deaf', 'my parents' attitude towards my boyfriend', 'not having a father', 'my father is an alcoholic', 'my father's violence', 'having parents who don't speak English', 'my father's unemployment', 'my father being away at sea for long periods', 'my mother having been to jail', 'my sister's [congenital] handicap', 'my sister being unmarried with a baby', 'my brother's bad kidneys', 'my parents just hate me', and 'I can't get over finding my father dead on the floor'.

These data suggest that although a majority of the Absentees blamed their institutions as being responsible for their initial and continued absences from school (see Chapter 4, page 44ff.) it is likely that the pupils' home circumstances and related psychological stress or worry were equally to blame. This is one of the many reasons why truancy and absenteeism must be viewed as multi-dimensional and multi-causal problems (see Chapter 1, pages 8–10). Researchers who simply investigate one or other facet of the topic will continue to a very large extent to waste their time.

Some of the longer responses made by the Absentees also give further insights into the daily lives of the sample.

'I hardly see my stepfather . . . he's got his own room and he's out most of the time. . . . They should be divorced really . . . they argue all the time' (fourth year girl).

'Good now. It wasn't good the year before when I was going out with a West Indian boy. It took a few months for my father to accept the situation. I was too frightened to say anything. . . . Maybe this contributed to my absence. . . . I wasn't concentrating in school' (fifth year girl).

'My mother gets on my nerves. She keeps nagging me . . . just because I keep getting up late. . . . Why shouldn't I watch television till closedown like them?' (fourth year girl).

'My father has a terrible temper. . . . He is often drunk. He hits us all then. . . . I just cry and scream . . . life is hell. . . . Sometimes it's OK' (fifth year girl).

These statements provide a good opportunity for another critical point to be made. The large experiential gap which exists between many teachers and the pupils they teach and often advise can be unhelpful and counter-productive. Teachers frequently offer advice on criteria which applied to them as children when the circumstances of such pupils as truants and absentees are radically different from their own. Much 'academic' and conformist advice can be viewed as irrelevant by pupils whose daily lives are a mixture of torment and despair. Such disadvantaged pupils often require 'practical' advice which keeps their heads above water, not in the clouds.

g   Parental Attitudes towards School

It is not surprising, in the light of the above and previous data, that highly significant differences were found between the perceptions of the Absentees and pupils in the two control groups on the extent of their parents' interest in their schoolwork. No fewer than 38 per cent of the Absentees firmly stated that their parents were not interested in their schoolwork. This proportion might have been even greater but for the natural loyalty shown by the Absentees towards their parents. Conversely, 95 and 82 per cent respectively of the Control Group 2 and 1 pupils considered that their parents were interested in their work at school.

When the views of the Absentees and control groups were sought on the number of visits made to school by one or both of their parents in the preceding 12 months, the differences between the three groups were magnified. The vast majority (83 per cent) of the parents of the Absentees had never voluntarily visited the school for any reason. Presumably this trait illustrated their lack of interest, as well as the desire to avoid the inevitable unfavourable comments from teachers which they knew they were bound to receive!

A majority (69 per cent) of the parents of Control Group 1 pupils had also never been to the school throughout the preceding 12 months. By contrast, a similar finding applied to only 19 per cent of the parents of the academic controls. Indeed, 45 per cent of these parents had visited their offspring's schools on two or more occasions in the previous year.

The unusual and volatile relationship which exists between one of the schools and some of the parents may partially have accounted for some of these large inter-group differences. For example, some of the parents of the Absentees objected to the school's frequent use of suspension and corporal punishment. Mrs Davies, the mother of one of the Absentees, told her daughter not to return to school until the headmaster had apologised because a senior teacher had sworn at her.

Implications for Practitioners

Most of the pupils in the study, including the Persistent Absentees, were extremely pleasant and co-operative at all times. Indeed, some of the Absentees' responses showed considerable insight into their own problems. Kelly's (1955) maxim that if a situation is beyond understanding, the views of the people most concerned should be sought, is as true today in education as ever.

The social anthropological approach used for the study was very successful in acquiring meaningful results. Potential researchers should note, however, that it is a very demanding and time consuming activity with few short cuts. Moreover, a discreet and tactful approach is needed.

Teachers as researchers and project staff may be pleasantly surprised by the frankness and honesty they will meet from teachers and pupils alike in such enquiries. Likewise, teachers need to remember that many absentees and truants do not get a great deal of support at home. Consequently, some of them are only too pleased to chat (and pour their hearts out) to interested third parties.

11

The Guidance of Truants

This chapter deals with a wide and complex field – the guidance and counselling of truants and school absentees. It is an area where there has been little research but about which we need to know a great deal more. It is abundantly clear, however, that most remedial processes with truants and persistent absentees are not very successful either inside or outside schools. Even truancy centres (Pugh, 1976; Grunsell, 1980), with all the care and thought which goes into their organisation and management, succeed too rarely in persuading their incumbents to return to their original or alternative state schools.

The simple fact is that most teachers and social workers do not have available the disproportionate amount of time which needs to be spent on and with children in non-attendance cases. Moreover, most teachers and social workers are not sufficiently qualified, skilful, trained or interested in this exceedingly difficult and intricate area. Given the generic structure of social work and the limitations placed on most teachers in their roles within schools, it is little wonder that many professionals merely skim the surface in their dealings with absentees and truants. In reality, because of heavy caseloads and the demands of teaching, it is quite common for schools and social workers to respond only to the worst or most immediate or necessary cases – the tip of the iceberg. Furthermore, there is clear and mounting evidence that unless absenteeism from school is caught in the early stages, it is likely to escalate until such time as the chronic or persistent stage is reached. It is fundamental that teachers, education welfare officers and social workers give more thought to the ways in which they detect and treat the onset of 'mitching'; this point will be dealt with further in Chapter 12.

First, however, it is essential to understand the difference between guidance and counselling. Guidance work is generally undertaken by unqualified staff such as teachers (heads of years, form teachers), acting in an administrative and 'caring' capacity. By contrast, counselling is a professional occupation undertaken by trained specialists (psychiatrists, educational psychologists, school counsellors) acting from a therapeutic standpoint. Too often, teachers and untrained social workers give themselves more credence than either their knowledge or competence merits and this can be dangerous. These people should never forget that actions and decisions which they take can directly or indirectly affect the quality of human lives.

Regrettably, there are too few trained specialists for the amount of clinical and non-clinical counselling advice needed to help with truants and absentees. Indeed, some 'professional' shortages reached the acute stage a long time ago as parents of handicapped children, amongst others, will readily testify. Indeed, after the initial boom when it was thought that large schools needed their own specialist workers, the appointment of qualified counsellors in schools has declined in many parts of Britain. There are several reasons for this including the economics of the situation and 'territorial' and quality aspects, especially as many headteachers resented having a member of their staff who knew more about certain pupils or issues than they themselves, or found few positive outcomes following the appointment of school counsellors. However, the result is that many schools have no professionally qualified first line of defence.

Counselling Truants

The evidence from published reports suggests that about three-quarters of truants given psychological treatment improve. Most psychologists recognise that there is no one standardised treatment or punishment for the behaviour, so that every truant is regarded as unique. The official policy followed by psychologists appears to be one of understanding the problem rather than coercion.

All too often schools assume that referring an absentee or truant to an educational psychologist or psychiatrist means the end of the problem for them. This is not usually the case but the attitude stems from a basic misunderstanding of the educational psychologist's role. Often, educational psychologists find themselves unable to do more than re-state the obvious and for some of them this is a source of professional frustration. While psychologists use a number of standardised tests with truants in the referral interviews and may suggest involving other agencies, for example, social workers or psychiatrists in particular cases, the fact remains that the involvement of educational psychologists rarely leads to long-term character and behavioural reformations on the part of the offender, but rather provides schools with confirmation of their diagnosis and further supporting or new evidence. I found that it is not unknown for even the most experienced psychologists to refuse to work with abusive and disruptive truants and absentees once they have been sworn at a few times! Sometimes, teachers forget that what they cannot accept is often also unacceptable to other professionals.

Taken overall, there has been an unequal amount of research from various professional standpoints on counselling and guidance with truants and absentees. For instance, comparatively more work has been done using behaviour modification techniques with both truants and phobics (Hersov, 1960a,b; Chazan, 1962; Kahn and Nursten, 1971; Yule, 1977; Yule *et al.*, 1980) than has been attempted using humanistic approaches.

Moreover, much of this research has been conducted in the United States, although researchers in Britain have played an important lead in combating and understanding school phobia or refusal (Frick, 1964; Hersov and Berg, 1980).

Galloway (1980a) has proposed three reasons for this state of affairs:

1   Truancy is usually regarded as just one aspect of a wide-ranging conduct disorder, whereas school refusal is often seen as the main expression of a neurotic disorder.
2   Conduct disorders are less amenable to clinic-based treatments than neurotic disorders, and have a worse prognosis (Levitt, 1963; Robins, 1966; Rutter and Madge, 1976).
3   Truants and their families may be less likely to co-operate in clinic-based intervention than school refusers who are referred for treatment, perhaps due to differences in social class attitudes towards professional help (Hersov, 1960a).

Hersov (1976, 1980) has reviewed the short- and long-term effects of using Skinner's principles of operant conditioning with school refusers and concluded that some of these techniques are more successful with some patients than with others. Although a variety of behaviour modification approaches have been successfully used with truants and absentees, it is not clear from the literature how much weight to give to these findings. Of the various behaviour modification methods used with truants and absentees, contingency contracting appears to be amongst the most popular (Harrop, 1983). One advantage of contingency contracts is that they can be tailor-made to deal with the specific problems of each truant or absentee. In Brook's research (1974), the contracts were devised by a school counsellor and involved a written contract between pupil, parent and school in which good school attendance was reinforced by previously agreed rewards. The pupils in Brook's experiment showed much improvement, but his cases seem to have been remarkably straightforward.

Further research is needed before too many conclusions are reached on this matter especially as many truancy or absenteeism cases are very far from straightforward. In any event, behaviour modification techniques are only a partial answer as they tend to be uneconomical, requiring one or more professionals to spend long hours with individual pupils or small groups. Such endeavours are unlikely to become universally popular until the long-term benefits which accrue are shown to be beyond doubt.

Social Work and Truancy

Psychologists and psychiatrists are not alone in neglecting research, especially multi-disciplinary approaches, into truancy and absenteeism. Social workers, teachers and education welfare officers have shown a similar diffidence – despite their favourable positions for undertaking this kind of work. Few projects have investigated the relationship between truancy and absenteeism and social work apart from the descriptive studies of Galloway, Ball and Seyd (1981a, b). Thus, comparatively little is known about what takes place when social workers are called in or intervene in cases which involve absentees and truants and/or their families. Without this certainty, it is extremely difficult to know which techniques and/or measures are effective in enabling new or chronic non-attenders to adjust and be successfully re-integrated into their schools. Generally speaking, as so little evaluative work has been undertaken into this vital function by social workers, it is extremely difficult for them to describe and be certain of 'good practice' even when it takes place. In this respect, more illuminative case studies need to be reported in the literature which have the potential to give a lead to others.

Despite these weaknesses, social workers are liable to come into contact with school absentees and truants for a variety of reasons, including referrals from court and schools (headteachers, counsellors, education welfare officers, heads of year – even form teachers), educational psychologists, psychiatrists, general practitioners, the police, local authorities and parents as well as a host of other possible sources. It is quite normal for a high proportion of social workers to come into contact with absentees and truants through their own caseloads and casework on or with other members of a family such as the parents, siblings or grandparents. The steady increase in social legislation for teenagers and young offenders which has been introduced through Parliament since the late 1960s has coincided with the current upsurge of interest and public concern in school absenteeism – especially truancy (Ekblom, 1979).

It has been suggested that the prevailing economic climate and the prospect of unemployment for young school-leavers could lead to an increase in school absenteeism rates and associated disorders, although research does not confirm or reject this possibility (Reid, 1983a). Certainly, there is renewed public concern about the development of a shadowy sub-culture of young people wandering loose in the city (Bird *et al.*, 1980; St John-Brooks, 1982).

It is extremely important that both new and experienced social workers have a clear picture of *all* the issues involved in school absenteeism and truancy (not just the social factors) even though for the time being they may have to devise their own 'treatment' (remedial) programmes. The latter task will not be easy, especially for young social workers who have to learn to combat and overcome the occasional prejudices of professionals from other disciplines as well as responding differently to each set of circumstances (Rose and Marshall, 1974; DHSS/Welsh Office, 1977). Even the most inexperienced social workers sometimes have to make difficult decisions requiring judgement, tact and considerable skill, guided only by the advice of their team leader.

My own research (Reid, 1982b, c) showed that a large proportion of my sample of Persistent Absentees (42 per cent) had a known involvement with the local social services department for a variety of reasons. These included cases of 'mental cruelty', 'absconding', 'child abuse', 'being out of parental control', 'psychiatric referrals', 'assault', 'appalling domestic circumstances', 'suspected handicaps', 'moral issues', 'unlawfully killing animals', 'suspected pupil victimisation', 'bullying', 'suspected child prostitution and incest', separation orders and a suspected school refusal case (later found unproven). This information was obtained from an educational social worker who had been placed on a full-time experimental project in one of the two schools in the study and she considered this proportion to be lower than the real figure if 'extended casework' was taken into account. Given that the schools in my study were located in exceedingly deprived catchment areas, it is hard to imagine any sort of guidelines which would enable social workers to overcome all the difficulties inherent in the aforementioned situations. Indeed, a further investigation into the records of the Persistent Absentees ascertained that a high proportion of them came from homes where they were the unfortunate victims of their parents' circumstances, perhaps with a parent in prison, missing (living in another region or abroad) or in debt, in addition to coming from low social class origins, large families and poor housing.

An examination of some of the multi-disciplinary or social service reports on the Persistent Absentees at School A substantiated the number of different aspects which are involved in many cases. For instance, a 15-year-old male Absentee was found to have had several special conferences called to discuss his case. One of these reports alone was 21 pages long and concluded with the following pessimistic statement:

> 'There seems to be nothing anyone can do to stop Tony's continued downward spiral. Originally, he was the victim of circumstances beyond his control but now he seems determined to make everyone else suffer for the fact. If something isn't done soon, I fear that anything might happen.'

Among the items highlighted in the report were: paternal violence toward mother (for which a prison sentence was being served), divorce, maternal alcoholism and co-habitation with different men, paternal debt (at one point all the family's furniture was sold and Tony and his two brothers and sister were taken into care – this was the first of three occasions), and fraternal truancy. Tony's own behaviour was far from exemplary. He once physically assaulted a teacher, repeatedly absconded from care, was prosecuted for theft and trespassing on private property and was widely suspected of participating in acts of criminal damage. In addition, he once imposed self-inflicted wounds upon himself, was notorious for being abusive to teachers when in school and for leaving the school premises during the day after either registering or participating in certain lessons. Finally, he was repeatedly rude to professional helpers and totally unable to conform or respond to any form of 'external' or 'internal' help offered by a variety of professionals and teachers alike. How young teachers or social workers can be expected to cope or respond to this situation without specialist training is far from clear – only an ardent optimist would believe that contingency contracting is the answer! Fortunately, cases like Tony's of aggressive, disruptive truants are in a small minority (Reid, 1984c).

Guidance within Schools

Like absentees and truants, each school is unique, a miniature society (Shipman, 1965). It is not surprising, therefore, that schools differ in the emphases which they attach to pastoral care and counselling and the ways in which they attempt to cope with their non-attendance problem.

Normally, teachers are less sympathetic towards some non-attenders such as truants than to others. Likewise, most pastoral teams tend to adopt overt disciplinary and custodial approaches with non-attenders, rather than empathetic and remedial ones. Reynolds and Murgatroyd (1977) have pointed out that many schools inadvertently reinforce through their 'clumsy' actions the precise deviant conduct which they are attempting to eradicate. For example, it goes without saying that when a member of staff is responsible for punishing pupils for their non-attendance, he or she is unlikely to be in the best position to help them. David Hargreaves's (1967) truism that secondary schools have one set of standards and criteria for their 'C' stream pupils and another for their 'A' stream is as true today as it was before comprehensives were introduced. The same applies to his statement that once teachers unfavourably categorise pupils as deviant it is very hard for these pupils to rid themselves of this label, irrespective of any reformation which subsequently takes place (see Chapter 6) (Hargreaves *et al.*, 1975).

In my own experience at Bicester School in the early seventies, the staff repeatedly found that both short- and long-term gains could be achieved by introducing personal tutoring and daily performance cards with chronic and disruptive cases of absenteeism (Reid, 1982d). However, despite maximum vigilance, these schemes all too rarely resulted in long-term improvements in pupil behaviour.

Staff Attitudes towards Intervention

(There is little doubt that wide attitudinal variations amongst staff on the best way to treat absentees and truants are apparent both from school to school and within schools. On no issue is this difference highlighted better than when teachers are asked how non-attenders should be treated or punished.)Responses are liable to range from the cane to unmitigated relief at the non-appearance of certain pupils! These feelings are exacerbated by the inherent variations which exist between the views, ethos, orientation and training of educationists and social workers. The plain truth is that too much depends upon individual ability, enthusiasm and personality. While social workers are generally sympathetic to the vast social problems which confront truants, many teachers tend to take the opposite stance as they believe that good attendance is the prime requisite for each pupil's educational progress and well-being at school.

Indeed, to speak bluntly, many teachers really think that social workers can do more harm than good and vice versa. It is for this reason that Davie (1977) argues that many more collaborative research projects should be undertaken between education and the social services. In particular, he thinks that ways should be sought to enable the interventions of teachers and social workers to complement rather than contradict one another.

Since the 1970s, a number of collaborative ventures and experiments have taken place between educationists and social workers (Rose and Marshall, 1974; Musgrave, 1975; Packwood, 1976; DHSS/Welsh Office, 1977; Morris, 1978; Robinson, 1978; Wolstenholme and Kolvin, 1980) and, in the mid and late seventies, a certain amount of research into the relationship between school absenteeism and truancy and pastoral care took place, mainly under the auspices of The University College of Swansea. Regrettably, since the retirement of Douglas Hamblin, much of this work seems to have dried up. Some worthwhile evidence was obtained from some small-scale studies with truants and school refusal cases which suggested that good counselling procedures used both by teachers and outside personnel could be effective in preventing, controlling and reducing non-attendance at school at least in the short-term (Law, 1973; Sassi, 1973; Cain, 1974; Beaumont, 1976; Tumelty, 1976; Kavanagh and Carroll, 1977). It is worth noting that most of these studies concentrated on secondary schools which ignored and tended to obviate the importance of the preventative potential of primary schools (Morgan, 1975).

An interesting and significant action-research project was carried out by Rose and Marshall (1974) in selected schools in Lancashire. They reported that attendance can be improved and delinquency reduced when counsellors or social workers are introduced into schools to work with and alongside teachers. But this is an issue fraught with controversy.

Special Units and 'Free' Schools

Two types of special units exist for dealing with difficult pupils (such as truants, phobics and disrupters): special units in ordinary schools and special units outside ordinary schools.

Berger and Mitchell (1978) reported the existence by the late seventies of over 200 special units in ordinary schools. The precise proportion of disruptive and/or truant pupils in these units is not yet known.

Early reports on these units were generally favourable but with some reservations (Boxall, 1973; Labon, 1973; Grunsell, 1978). However, special units in ordinary schools have continued to be a contentious issue.

Some educationists consider that the primary thrust of these units should be therapy, others deterrence. Lodge (1977) argues that there is a need to protect the majority from the conduct and influence of the deviant minority through the use of special unit schemes. Different educationists have stressed the social potential of these special units, particularly their ability to respond to the individual requirements of children with special needs (Jones, N., 1974).

Galloway (1980a) suggests that headteachers traditionally oppose the introduction of any form of unit for absentee or disruptive pupils for three reasons:

1 The existence of such a unit tends to 'normalise' deviant behaviour in the eyes of some sections of the population, and thus reduces the potential influences of group pressure from the conforming majority.
2 It is as unsound educationally to separate children with behavioural disorders from their peers as it is to cream off the academic elite into grammar schools.
3 The units reduce the commitment of class teachers and subject teachers to handle problems themselves. Removing pupils to special units tends to make certain teachers reluctant to co-operate when deviant pupils return from specialist units and are put back into ordinary classrooms. Certainly, some teachers welcome the 'safety valve' which is afforded by special units as it gives them a break from unruly pupils and an opportunity to stabilise their relationship with the rest of the form. It may also help to reduce some teachers' levels of stress.

The emergence of a number of special units outside ordinary schools is comparatively well documented, sometimes in a kind of descriptive and almost evangelical fashion (Lane, 1977; Lane and Millar, 1977; Grunsell, 1978; NACRO, 1978). Most of the units or centres are organised on an *ad hoc* basis – some catering specifically for truants and absentees, others looking after the small 'hard core' of rebels, disrupters and delinquents who can be found in many secondary schools, particularly in inner city regions such as Liverpool and London. Some of the units are organised by local education authorities and run by teachers; others come under the aegis of the social services, frequently including teachers seconded from the education departments on their staff. In this connection, it is worth noting that the Pack Committee recommended the provision of day units for truants rather than residential facilities as being most appropriate in non-attendance cases (Scottish Education Department, 1977).

It is difficult to generalise about these units as so many of them incorporate novel features into their 'constitutions' and are notable for the amount of freedom given to the students. In some 'free' schools and specialist units, there appears to be a consensus that formulating too many rules for students to observe militates against favourable outcomes and relaxed atmospheres.

Rowan (1976) has indicated that children are accepted into outside units provided they remain on the registers of their ordinary school, to which it is hoped they will eventually return, although in practice this is seldom achieved. Some units specifically encourage adults who have been in trouble as adolescents to collaborate in the management, teaching and curriculum of their centres. Others do not encourage formal curricula of any sort but allow a kind of 'free for all' situation to develop in the hope that this will lead to meaningful activity on the part of the pupils. With the exception of the Hungerford Centre in London (Lane, 1977, Lane and Millar, 1977) which uses a system of short-term contingency contracts devised by the child and the centre's staff together, few useful evaluative accounts of the work of these units exist.

Further research is needed into the structure, organisation and effectiveness of both special units within ordinary schools and those outside the mainstream. Until such work is undertaken, doubt will always remain about their real potential, usefulness and effectiveness. A longitudinal or follow-up study would be especially valuable in looking at the outcome of incumbents of special units some years after leaving school.

Implications for Practitioners

The prime requisite for both social workers and teachers is to recognise their limitations in dealing with those cases which require expert advice and/or help. Social workers and teachers need to learn to be able to detect symptoms which indicate or suggest that skilled specialist advice or help is needed. As the incidence of school refusal is so low (Rutter *et al.*, 1970), most social workers and teachers will never come across this type of case in their entire careers. If, however, a social worker or teacher suspects that for any reason a pupil is a possible school refusal case, he or she should refer the pupil immediately through the appropriate channels. As informed advice is not always readily forthcoming within schools and social service departments, teachers and social workers should consult for preliminary information one of a variety of texts available on the subject (Kahn *et al.*, 1981; Hersov and Berg, 1980).

It is crucial that both teachers and social workers are aware of the fundamental variations which exist between school refusal and truancy cases lest they do serious damage. The former, for example, is an emotional disorder whereas the latter is a behavioural disorder. Fortunately, there are long established and easily detectable differences between the genesis, treatment and prognosis of the two traits which are at opposite ends of the continuum. The prime requisite when dealing with school refusal cases is often to relieve the pupils from undue mental pressure, frequently associated with such factors as high intelligence, over-enthusiastic parents and self-imposed anxiety. By contrast, truancy cases tend to pose a different problem – how to motivate the pupil who has constantly and deliberately missed school to return to the fold. Nevertheless, even in cases of truancy, chronic absenteeism and parental-condoned absence, there are times when referral to outside agencies and specialist help is required – for example, when the reason for the non-attendance indicates some form of serious home, social, psychological or school-related problems. Sometimes absentees' genuine concern about attending school needs to be resolved before they can realistically be expected to adjust and re-integrate into school life. Without such positive action, subsequent events may prove monotonously repetitive and unsuccessful. For example, I found that it is not unusual for an absentee to build a comparatively minor incident into major proportions.

Sometimes schools as well as absentees need to change to accommodate individual circumstances. As mentioned previously, these changes can be minimal, a change of form, timetable, teacher, school or perhaps additional help with such items as reading, writing and arithmetic. If schools are not prepared to change to meet their needy pupils, should we really expect deprived pupils to change?

Looking to the future, ways need to be found to involve more social workers and teachers in meaningful collaborative ventures. The gulf between the two professions continues to be as great as ever and must be bridged (Skinner *et al.*, 1983). This will not be easy without further research into 'good practice'. Moreover, given the present heavy caseloads and demands on social workers and teachers' time (large classes and so on), there is some distance to go before sound theory can be put into practice. Few headteachers will or can be expected to release staff to engage in multi-disciplinary case conferences on persistent absentees when they are unable to find suitable temporary replacements. Given existing policies, most headteachers will inevitably see such involvement as an expensive waste of scarce resources. Similarly, administrators in both the social services and education departments tend to need convincing that these time consuming activities are likely to bring forth positive results for all concerned in the enterprise. In this respect, social workers and teachers must be realistic; there is a considerable gap between a good idea being conceived and its acceptance by administrators, schools, parents and the absentees themselves.

Many professionals involved with truants and absentees continue to be plagued by a longstanding problem. Parents of truants and persistent absentees are often not the most co-operative or dependable of people. Social workers and teachers need to educate parents to accept the notion that regular attendance at school is essential for the well-being of their offspring. But this is not easy with certain categories of parent, especially those who are disinterested in their children's schooling.

Notwithstanding the problems mentioned above, a number of positive measures could be taken now to improve substantially the chances of successful outcomes being achieved when social workers intervene or are called into truancy cases. There is, for example, little doubt that the basic knowledge which social workers have about truancy and school absentee-ism is frequently inadequate. Indeed, the topic appears to be omitted from the initial (and in-service) curriculum of many social workers' training courses. It should become an essential requirement that all social workers be given a course on this topic either in their initial or in-service program-mes. When the subject is included on social workers' course schedules, it often concentrates on only the legal and social aspects of the problem. Although these aspects are especially relevant to social work, the related psychological, institutional and educational aspects are just as important.

Regrettably, this omission is not solely confined to social work; a parallel situation exists in teaching. Consequently, many social workers and teachers think they know a great deal more about the reasons and remedial programmes available in truancy cases than they do. This is a potentially dangerous situation in terms of human welfare.

Given the present unsatisfactory situation, local authorities should begin to get together to devise their own multi-disciplinary schemes of training which enable social workers and teachers to appreciate each other's specialist field. This idea is not new (DHSS/Welsh Office, 1977). So far, however, despite a considerable amount having been written on the subject, in many regions little more than lip service has been paid to this concept for a variety of reasons, including the shortages of resources, manpower and related administrative difficulties. If and when these constraints are lifted, the aim of the training should be threefold:

- to develop and extend the horizons of teachers and social workers: teachers could do some social work and vice versa;
- to end or lessen the philosophical and practical divisions between the two professions which often surface in 'territorial' disputes (Smithells, 1977);
- to promote good inter-disciplinary co-operation based on mutual understanding and need.

Social workers should be encouraged to 'major' in school absenteeism and/or related problems in just the same way as they currently specialise in 'handicap', 'care', and 'geriatric' work within the overall generic framework. The same should happen within schools. Every school should have at least one expert on absenteeism on the staff. This is especially important in such regions as South Wales, Scotland and industrial con-urbations where absenteeism is recognised as a substantial and disprop-ortionate problem.

12

Towards Good Practice

There is, of course, no ready made panacea to help schools overcome their absenteeism 'problem'. Hard work and a willingness to persist over a period of time are the two commodities most needed if schools are to succeed in this objective.

Unfortunately, at present there are too few accounts available which cite good practice within schools. Two notable exceptions are the chapter by Jones, A. (1980) on Vauxhall Manor School's policies and my own (Reid, 1982d) version of preventative and remedial techniques at Bicester (see pages 121–2). Given that most schools tend to be judged by their external examination results rather than the implementation of successful policies to combat non-attendance, it is hardly surprising that many schools choose to emphasise the former.

Nevertheless, 'enforced' changes may soon be on the way. Evidence is mounting to show that serious 'local' stigmas are created when unfavourable comments in HMI reports are published and publicised. This may be one of the positive aspects of having HMI school visitation reports published and readily available to the general public, although perhaps not all headteachers would agree!

Leadership

Good practice in schools begins with a firm lead from the head and permeates down through the system to the deputies, heads of year and department to the form teacher. Every member of staff has an important part to play in the prevention of absenteeism. Condoning absenteeism by omission or neglect is a clear sign to absentees that their school really does not care about them.

To be frank, in large secondary schools heads of year, counsellors and education welfare officers have far too much to do to spend time on every instance of new or prolonged absence without adequate support from heads of department and form teachers. It is no use heads of department in schools pleading that they only have an academic leadership function to fulfil. Every teacher has a pastoral facet to his or her role in just the same way that every teacher is a teacher of maths and English. Before pastoral teams became the norm in secondary schools, most staff accepted their pastoral responsibilities willingly. This was merely an extension of their overall professional responsibilities.

The Philosophy of Schools

When a school gets its policies right a lot can be done to prevent, forestall and combat absenteeism. It is not difficult to detect either occasional, persistent or initial non-attendance; it is an essential prerequisite that a good pastoral system does so. Early detection must be a major feature and emphasis of any scheme. Once detected, the problem should be followed up as soon as possible in the best interests of all concerned, not least the pupils. In the long run, a major drive to prevent and overcome initial non-attendance makes everyone's life easier. Heads of year, for instance, should be able to account for every pupil under their care at all times throughout a school day. But this is not always the case. At one secondary school I visited, I counted over 60 pupils who were on the school premises but not in class or under close supervision during timetabled teaching time.

The Role of Education Welfare Officers within Schools

The status of the education welfare officer within school warrants further consideration. Far too many education welfare officers feel that they are peripheral rather than integral members of staff. Some, for example, are treated as non-professionals by teachers, certainly not as equals. Some are expected to stay out of staff common rooms, take coffee with secretarial staff and make appointments to see teachers. Some are refused access to crucial reports from social workers, educational psychologists and psychiatrists even when they are dealing with a particular case. This is ridiculous and such bad and antiquated practice should cease altogether. When bad practice pertains in schools, teachers should not be surprised when they confront disillusioned, ineffective and inefficient education welfare officers. Sometimes teachers as well as pupils give credence to the notion that education welfare officers are mere 'boardy-men' with their attitudes to someone who in effect is a fellow professional.

Headteachers, deputies and heads of year need to stress the fundamental value of education welfare officers to schools, not least in making pastoral systems effective. It goes without saying that if schools gave their education welfare officers more help and support, the pupils might follow suit.

Although in some parts of Britain local headteachers already meet once or twice a term to discuss mutual problems, headteachers in other parts should be encouraged to do so. Matters for discussion should include absenteeism and the effective role of education welfare officers in schools. In this way a greater uniformity in approach could be achieved. Too many education welfare officers are currently handicapped because the school they are in follows different policies from school B, C or D in the same region. The efficiency of education welfare officers can also be reduced by neglect or disinterest amongst senior staff towards non-attendance cases, by 'tensions' between social workers and schools, and by the haphazard verdicts reached in the courts.

The Bicester Scheme

The Bicester Scheme, originally introduced by John Sharp, Margaret Maden and Harry Hovard is very time consuming, but effective. It is one of a host of schemes which are operated by different schools but space restrictions preclude discussing them all here. In the Bicester format, the steps are sub-divided into three stages: daily, weekly and periodic checks which take place fairly regularly.

Daily Measures
1 All staff participate in the scheme to a greater or lesser extent.
2 Form registers are marked at the beginning of the morning and afternoon sessions as per normal practice.
3 In the morning registration period, all pupils marked absent are recorded on appropriate forms. One copy of this form is then taken immediately to the head of year while a second is retained by a class monitor.
4 At the start of each lesson, the class monitor gives the teacher the sheets containing the list of absentees. A form register is called and checked alongside the absentee form. Any absences not recorded on the list are notified to the head of year without delay. The head of year responds to this new information at once by instigating on-site checks, phoning parents or taking whatever action he or she deems necessary.
5 At the end of the day all the appropriate information is collated and disseminated by the heads of year to the staff, including the education welfare officer and school counsellor.

Weekly Measures
1 Regular progress reports on persistent absentees are made. Action taken as a result of specific lesson absences is recorded.
2 Heads of year and senior staff meet to discuss the prevailing situation and monitor progress. Appropriate remedial action is introduced for specific offenders.

Measures taken Periodically
1 Progress reports are given to staff through year and staff meetings, bulletins and notices pinned to the daily and weekly notice-boards.
2 The implementation of special pupil schemes is reported and the effects of these schemes monitored.
3 The practice of the entire system is reviewed periodically and amended as needed.

This process has been in operation at Bicester since the early seventies; the school's average daily attendance is now 92 per cent, an improvement of 15 per cent being obtained within the first three years. There is no doubt that this is a remarkable achievement given the special problems which the school has to cope with, partly as a result of its difficult catchment area and large numbers of pupils with social problems of one kind or another caused by such factors as disadvantaged home backgrounds. The long-term improvement must be credited to the entire staff since it has only been achieved through their conscientious and concerted efforts. They have always had to balance the gains to be had with the acknowledged losses in available teaching time.

The concept and ensuing policy originally grew out of need. Today, the scheme survives because it has become one way for the staff to communicate their general concern for their pupils' welfare to the pupils themselves and their parents, and also to enforce good attendance habits. Moreover, the staff as a whole have been made aware that non-attendance at school can be an early warning for a vast array of potentially more serious problems. Hence, professionals at Bicester now accept that every member of staff from the form teacher upwards has a crucial role to play in the school's pastoral care systems and in the prevention of absenteeism and related problems.

Through their own diligence and determination the staff at Bicester have managed to turn a difficult problem to their advantage. Until further research into good practices is undertaken, there is no reason why other schools should not follow Bicester's lead. It is vitally important, however, that when such schemes are implemented, the whole staff are involved and prepared to ensure that the operation works, not only at its inception, but later when the effects of the policies have begun to bite and the staff see the scheme as less necessary and more of a chore.

Implications for Practitioners

Heads of department and senior staff must be prepared to teach less able and difficult lower ability, often non-examination, forms. In far too many schools, capable and experienced teachers manage to avoid these kinds of forms year after year under the guise that their particular skills are needed for the academic bands. This means that the least well qualified and experienced staff tend to teach 5K and 4X. Staff should not then feel too surprised if some of their most disadvantaged pupils feel poorly treated; after all, comparatively speaking, they are right!

If the Bicester scheme was introduced nationwide, much specific lesson 'truancy' and other covert activities inside schools would be dramatically curtailed. Moreover, staff would start to accumulate some real evidence on what they as teachers and their schools as caring institutions could do to help some of their most disadvantaged pupils to overcome their personal and educational problems. While such vigilance may not find favour in every quarter (such as the smoker's union!), it would help to break down some of the traditional gulf which exists between teachers and pupils. Most pupils naturally respect staff who take an interest in their welfare and the welfare of their peers.

13
Truancy and Adult Life

As with many other emotional disorders of childhood, the long-term prognosis for school refusers in adult life is good. Although estimates vary, the success rate for persuading refusers to return to school appears to be about 60 per cent (Berg, 1980). In very young children the problem is generally short lived (Frick, 1964; Miller *et al.*, 1972) but for older children the condition can be more worrying. However, apart from a limited number of very disturbed pupils when the problem has proved insoluble despite all the efforts at treatment, most researchers believe that the vast majority of school refusers generally adjust well in their adult lives and become good citizens. Nevertheless, Tyrer and Tyrer's important (1974) study of some 240 psychiatric patients suggested, contrary to much previous work, that there may be a link between childhood and adult disorders. They concluded that some children with problems of school refusal may be at risk in adult life. Pritchard and Graham reported in 1966 that adult patients who had attended both child and adult psychiatric departments of the same hospital usually showed a similar type of disorder to the one they were treated for as children.

There are considerable differences between the outlook for truants when compared with school refusers. Tyerman (1965), without providing any evidence, suggests that about three-quarters of truants referred to educational psychologists subsequently show improvement in behaviour and/or attendance. Other studies, however, have consistently found that truancy and school absenteeism are early warning signs of more serious problems in adult life, such as criminal activities, inability to settle into the routine of work and/or marriage and isolationism (Pitts and Simon, 1954; Stott and Wilson, 1968; Farrington, 1976).

It seems that the truants and absentees who are referred to educational psychologists by schools are often the most serious cases, frequently truant delinquents. The long-term prognosis for these pupils is much worse than for occasional absentees. Children with anti-social and conduct disorders referred to child guidance clinics, educational psychologists or psychiatrists are significantly more likely to develop certain types of personality disorders in adult life than other groups of children (Robins, 1966). For this reason, Rutter (1972) has suggested that it should be routine in psychiatric referrals to enquire into the patient's history of school attendance as he believes this may provide more meaningful information than the time-honoured questions about neurotic traits in

childhood. By implication, he believes that questions about school attendance may prove to be one of the best predictors of later psychiatric
disturbance.

In these connections, the work of Robins and Ratcliff (1980) is very
important. They undertook a longitudinal study of 235 adult black males
born in St Louis between 1930 and 1934, who attended public schools for
at least six years and had intelligence quotients above the median. They
found that:

1   elementary school truancy, often beginning in the first grade, forecasts
    continued truancy in high school, particularly amongst those who
    display other kinds of deviant behaviour, such as early drinking, early
    sexual activity and illicit drug use, and those who are known to be
    delinquents;
2   both elementary and high school truancy are associated with dropping
    out of school before completing secondary education and with low
    earnings as an adult;
3   high school truancy is strongly related to a variety of adult deviant
    behaviours and somewhat associated with psychological disturbance.

Although the authors do not know how applicable these findings might
be outside the US, they suspect that for males they could be considerably
generalised. It is interesting that in another paper written in the US,
Robins, Ratcliff and West (1979) showed that pupils who play truant from
elementary school tend to marry girls who played truant at a similar age
and they then have sons and daughters who also play truant, thereby
perpetuating a truancy-syndrome into the next generation. These findings
accord well with my own work which suggests that in some ways male and
female non-attenders have more in common with one another than with
good attenders (see Chapters 6 and 7, pages 64–6 and 72–4).

Hathaway *et al.* (1969) found that school dropouts in the US are more
likely to have higher separation and divorce rates, larger families, lower
social mobility and to be caught up in the 'poverty trap' than the 'normal'
population. For girls, 'dropping out' was found to be less catastrophic
than for boys.

In all cases of absenteeism, the earlier the treatment or remedial process
is initiated the better the outlook and the quicker the disappearance of the
symptoms (Herbert, 1974). If treatment is delayed, the undesirable side
effects may spiral (Andriola, 1943, 1946; Teicher, 1973). There is clear
evidence that those schools which fail to implement satisfactory early
warning systems inadvertently encourage initial absences to ferment and
grow. Davie (1972), for example, found that pupils who begin to miss
school at the age of seven generally continue to skip school at the age of
11.

While truancy and absenteeism present good opportunities for early
intervention, there is nothing to suggest that later intervention is useless –
casework may just be more difficult. Robins and Ratcliff (1980) report that

boys who complete their high school education despite a record of truancy, have considerably better adult outcomes than those whose truancy led them to drop out of school. This finding indicates that it is worth experimenting with methods to encourage even persistent absentees and the less able population to complete their secondary schooling. Much more research is needed into this important question; it is not known, for example, whether those who succeed at school and in adult life despite histories of truancy or absenteeism have special personal qualities, favourable home backgrounds and/or more positive school support than their counterparts who fail.

The Career Aspirations of Persistent Absentees

Previously unpublished data collated from my own study suggest that pupils' long-term career aspirations affect their attitudes towards their schools and teachers. The Persistent Absentees and two control groups were asked what careers and/or jobs they hoped to go into upon leaving school. Analysis of these data showed that significantly more of the Absentees and their controls from the same forms hoped to obtain employment in unskilled or semi-skilled work, in occupations where career openings are decreasing and likely to diminish further in the future. By contrast, the academic controls generally aspired to enter higher or further education, the professions or prestigious technical occupations. Consequently, both the Absentees and matching controls placed considerable emphasis upon the vocational importance of such subjects as mathematics and English which, they recognised, could influence their opportunities to find suitable employment when they left school at 16.

Evidence obtained from their interviews suggested that when the Absentees and matching controls perceived they were doing badly in these key subjects, or were dissatisfied with either the teaching or their teachers, then this proved a considerable source of bitterness to them, often exacerbating their disaffection and alienation from school. Unlike their academic peers, these pupils were unable or unwilling to bring parental pressure to bear upon the school. Undoubtedly, this was partially because they knew or feared that such parental intervention would inevitably be used to discuss other matters like their classroom behaviour or non-attendance. In fact, any action which they took of their own volition in terms of group or individual complaints usually only got them into further trouble. Andrew, 15, for example, claimed that he was being victimised by a teacher at his school because he complained about her inability to teach or help him with his reading in class. He claimed that he was desperate to learn to read and his inability to do so lay behind much of his frustration in school, culminating in his disruptive conduct in certain classes and, eventually, his persistent absenteeism.

It is my own firm opinion that the link between the curriculum and teaching standards in school is so obvious and fundamental that the dearth of evidence into this relationship is a clear indictment of much previous research. In these times, there is also a strong case for introducing careers guidance and careers lessons much earlier than often happens currently. If potential disrupters and absentees were fully aware of the long-term consequences of their actions, they might think twice. Schools, too, should have an onus placed on them to give as much help and careers guidance to their less fortunate pupils as to those who are gifted. This could be less easy than it sounds. In my experience, the quality and kind of vocational guidance which is offered in secondary schools often leaves a great deal to be desired.

Non-attendance at School and Work

The factors associated with adult absenteeism from work have been widely investigated for a considerable period of time. There is, however, some imbalance between the number of studies which have been undertaken into different kinds of occupations; for example, more research has been conducted into absenteeism from work amongst manual and semi-skilled than professional workers.

A few projects have been undertaken into the link between school absenteeism and absenteeism from work in adult life (Lummis, 1946; Cherry, 1976; Gray *et al.*, 1980). These show that the outlook for absentees and dropouts from school is far from favourable (Bienstock, 1967; Swanstrom, 1967; Coombs and Cooley, 1968; Hathaway *et al.*, 1969; Bachman *et al.*, 1971).

Cherry (1976) used the National Children's Bureau longitudinal data to investigate the antecedents of persistent job changing in the early years of work. She found that:

1   poor attendance at school is one of three significant predictors of job instability amongst the 15–18 age group; the other two are teacher ratings of behaviour and levels of general intelligence;
2   poor attendance at school is related to frequent changes of job which tend to persist for up to eight years to the age of 26;
3   poor school attendance and job instability are associated to a significant degree with a variety of personal problems: broken marriages, unemployment, psychiatric disorder and having illegitimate children.

It is interesting that Cherry found that while school absenteeism is related to frequent job changing and job dissatisfaction, it is not associated with lower earnings. Indeed, she reported that adults with personal problems who change jobs persistently sometimes actually earn more than those who remain loyal to their original employer.

Sheila Mitchell (1972) also reported that boys who had a bad school attendance record experience more frequent changes of job and lower levels of job satisfaction than those who have been good attenders at school. Boys who have histories of absenteeism from school also tend to be dissatisfied with their existing employment. Indeed, many of them yearned to do something different, though not necessarily better, at the time of their interviews. Conversely, the majority of boys who had good attendance records at school felt reasonably satisfied at work and aspired to continue in their present employment for at least the following two years.

The work of Gray *et al.* (1980) has shown that absenteeism from school has several short-term consequences for teachers as well as non-attenders because:

a   absentees are much more unlikely to remain at school after the age of 16 and move into the sixth form;
b   absentees are likely to leave school at the first possible opportunity before taking national examinations;
c   absentees are likely to achieve a lower level of scholastic attainment in public examinations than good attenders.

Illegal Employment

Educationists and social workers have shown a marked concern over the question of school children who work illegally in their spare time or during school hours (Johnson *et al.*, 1980). For instance, the Newsom Report (1963) found (before the school-leaving age was raised to 16) that 42 per cent of boys and 16 per cent of girls in the 14 plus age group in secondary modern schools were engaged in some kind of gainful employment. Given recent and existing social and economic pressure, these percentages may even have increased.

Local education authorities have certain duties under the Employment of Children Act, 1973. Children under 13 may not be employed, and older pupils of compulsory school age may take employment only under prescribed conditions.

On days on which he is required to attend school, a child may not be employed before the end of school hours, nor for more than two hours. He may not be employed for more than two hours on a Sunday, nor before seven o'clock in the morning, nor after seven o'clock at night on any day. The nature of the employment must be such that he is not required to lift, carry or move anything so heavy as to be likely to cause him injury (Barrell, 1978).

Terry

Terry was a 14-year-old boy who repeatedly missed school when he was in my form in the early seventies. After a while I noticed that when he did attend school he frequently appeared to be half-asleep. Investigation showed that he assisted his father on a milk round every morning before school, getting up at four o'clock. In the early evenings he did a newspaper round and another one at the weekends. Eventually tiredness led Terry to display some strange behaviour when in school (falling asleep in lessons, jumping out of windows in the middle of a class, hurling abuse at teachers – this was completely out of character – and ignoring his friends). These activities were taken as signs of 'pleas for help' and it was not long before the school fully investigated his circumstances and, after consultations with his parents, limited his out of school activities in term time and introduced some booster programmes to enable him to catch up on his work.

Pupil Fantasy

Children, like adults, have aspirations, dreams and ambitions. Nevertheless, the fascinating subject of pupils' fantasies has tended to be a neglected area in the literature, possibly because of the difficulties surrounding the gathering and quantification of these kind of data.

For this reason, I asked the Persistent Absentees and two control groups what they would like to do if they could choose anything. An analysis of these data showed that by and large the pupils in the three groups shared roughly similar dreams but with one subtle difference.

Most of the pupils had cultural, recreational or social aspirations (to be a film star, pop singer or professional footballer). The only revealing and major difference was that 22 per cent of the Absentees had career fantasies (to be a welder, bricklayer, mechanic) compared with only seven and two per cent of Control Groups 1 and 2 respectively. Presumably, this difference highlights the fact that some poor attenders 'dream' of finding good jobs because inwardly they know that the odds are stacked against them – a compensatory aspiration.

Implications for Practitioners

At the time of writing (1985), several new DES initiatives are beginning to be taken for young school-leavers which could have marked effects upon outcomes for truants and absentees and their immediate post-school experience. Some experiments are already being carried out on the use of pupil profile systems for school-leavers which give more detailed personal and school biographical details to potential employers than has previously been the case. Some local education authorities are beginning to revert to the practice of providing school-leaving certificates for all school-leavers. These moves have sparked off considerable public interest and could act as a deterrent to absenteeism from school. Clearly, the outlook for pupils who miss some or a great deal of their schooling is now more serious than ever given the dearth of opportunities for long-term employment in manual and semi-skilled occupations. To what extent the Technical and Vocational Educational Initiative (TVEI) will cater for such groups as absentees is a matter which only time will show. The possibility remains, however, that work placement and other related schemes are one way of making non-attenders more interested in educational practices, especially those who are disenchanted with their school curriculum.

14

Conclusions and Prospective Outlook

Summary of Existing Knowledge

The marked tendency for absentees and truants to come from unsupportive and deprived home and social backgrounds is well known and is well documented. By contrast, a great deal more information needs to be obtained about the psychological and institutional processes which lead some pupils to withdraw and continue to miss school.

As a result, it is not yet feasible to answer the following fundamental question: 'Why does pupil A miss school when pupil B from the same form and a roughly similar home and social background is a good attender?'

Previous writers have tended to suggest that the answer largely lies in parental apathy and the absence of positive parental support or interest in education, as well as the pupils' social and home disadvantages. However, this ignores the important contribution made by the schools and the pupils' own temperaments and personalities. Research conducted in the mid to late seventies and early eighties has re-emphasised the importance of socio-educational (Reynolds *et al.*, 1980), socio-psychological (Galloway *et al.*, 1982), psychological (Reid, 1982a), institutional (Reynolds *et al.*, 1980) and multi-disciplinary (Reid, 1984a) facets in the genesis and continuation of school absenteeism and truancy. Although these pioneer studies have pointed the way forward, considerably more work is necessary before any certainty can be attributed to the precise features of schools which contribute to and foster absenteeism. In particular, much more educational research is needed into the crucial link which exists between teachers, teaching styles, the curriculum, discipline, school rules and pastoral care systems and absenteeism. Similarly, further social and psychological studies are needed in the field of personality, alienation, disaffection, pupil behaviour and peer group relationships, that can be related to those features of schooling which encourage or discourage attendance.

To date, the evidence clearly suggests that multi-disciplinary aspects are involved in the related phenomena of absenteeism and truancy from school. Absentees and truants tend to come from unfavourable and unsupportive home backgrounds, *and* have low social class origins, *and* display psychological or behavioural problems of one kind or another, *and* have lower intellectual levels than the average child, *and* have a number of adjustment and learning difficulties in school, *and* have fewer friends than many of their peers, *and* have poorer teacher–pupil relationships, *and* find difficulties in conforming to the rules and regulations imposed by schools.

Unfortunately, in spite of the dearth of both multi-disciplinary and inter-disciplinary studies, too little is known about the links between the home, social, psychological and institutional factors involved in truancy and absenteeism as well as the inter-agency links between professionals who work with truants and absentees in the health and social services and educational professionals, particularly the latter two. There is a mass of work waiting to be done in these fields using both quantitative and qualitative approaches and large- and small-scale samples.

Of one thing we can be certain – teachers, counsellors, educational psychologists, social workers and other professionals tend not to be very successful in compelling chronic absentees and truants to return to and remain in their schools once they have been detected. Not only do intervention and therapeutic approaches generally fail, they are usually applied too late, without adequate thought, and too often for the wrong reasons: the institution's or state's wishes rather than the absentees' genuine needs. Much more imaginative casework with truants and absentees is required both in and out of schools.

Jane

Jane, 15, was the only child in a one parent family. She was a good attender at primary school, only infrequently missing school for such reasons as illness. But shortly after her transfer to the local comprehensive, she began 'mitching' for days on end. By the age of 13, she was regarded as a chronic absentee by the school and her mother was prosecuted. At first, Jane's mother condoned her daughter's non-attendance because she enjoyed her company at home. After her first court appearance, however, her mother's attitude changed completely and she became totally unreceptive to her daughter's whims. Thereafter, Jane flirted with the idea of attending school regularly but shortly afterwards she had a major row with her form teacher and the deputy headteacher over her failure to wear the proper school uniform. This incensed Jane and began to make her bitter because she felt the school authorities could have shown more consideration, especially as they knew her parents were divorced and her mother relied heavily on social security and child benefit. Immediately after the argument, Jane again started to miss school regularly, spending much of her time at a friend's house. Jane's mother only discovered this renewed escalation after a visit from the school's education welfare officer.

Work with Jane showed her to have below average intelligence, very low self-esteem and a low academic self-concept, reasonable conduct and a generally pleasant disposition and personality – a 'traditional' absentee (see Chapter 4). She confessed to feeling highly alienated from her school because of its size, its 'petty' regulations and the attitudes of the staff, in particular one senior teacher. Nevertheless, whilst she cared little for the school, she specifically mentioned that she did not hate or dislike her teachers. Rather, she felt that many of her teachers were as much trapped by the 'system' as she was herself. She was, however, repeatedly critical of the staff's general teaching and the content of many of her lessons which she regarded as a 'waste of time'. Jane believed fervently that none of the staff, from her form teacher upwards, had her best interests at heart. She continually mentioned how unusual it was for any teacher to give her any individual attention in lessons. Moreover, she was scathing about the school's insensitivity at being unable to make any allowances for her given her own and her mother's difficult social circumstances. On one occasion, she mentioned her wish to learn to read better and to write well so that she could find a good job. On another, she burst into tears when she described what a teacher had said to her mother on a rare school visit about her lack of potential, her attendance and her attitude.

Discussion with appropriate staff suggested that they felt that the blame for Jane's non-attendance could be laid on her home circumstances. They regarded themselves and the policies of their school as being blameless for any of her absenteeism, despite Jane's insistence that she would have attended school regularly if she believed the school really cared for her welfare, if more imaginative and more relevant lessons were provided and if the school was less punitive about what she regarded as petty rules and regulations.

My own subjective assessment of the facts is that no one emerged with any credit from the case. Certainly, Jane's circumstances were far from insurmountable. Indeed, her non-attendance should never have been allowed to graduate from the initial to the occasional and persistent stages.

Let us look closely at this case. The staff at the school did the minimum because of their philosophy and policies, the large number of absentees and related problems which they had to cater for in a difficult catchment area, and their wholehearted conviction that the home rather than the school was to blame for Jane's behaviour. The social services did the minimum because they were far too busy dealing with more urgent cases. Jane's mother made a potentially difficult situation much worse by not being sufficiently firm at the beginning and by changing horse in mid-stream. Similarly, Jane did not help herself either by regular attendance or by expounding her real feelings to staff at the school.

An analysis of the facts suggests that she is well on the way to becoming one of life's losers. Her absenteeism has managed only to reinforce her already low self-concept, limited academic ability and lack of social prestige in the community – hardly credentials likely to find her gainful and stimulating employment or to enable her to climb the social ladder.

Jane's circumstances mirror the prevailing lack of imagination which exemplifies casework with truants and school absentees in many schools. These deficiencies are magnified to some extent by time constraints, workloads, professional shortages and inadequate initial and in-service training programmes in teaching, social work, educational psychology and educational welfare work. Unless and until this situation vastly improves, remedial work with truants and absentees is likely to continue to be *ad hoc*, haphazard and not very successful.

Given the *in loco parentis* concept which is strictly interpreted by the courts in children's cases, as well as the overwhelming evidence linking truancy and absenteeism with delinquent and maladjusted behaviour, many headteachers must lie awake in their beds wondering whether they and their schools are liable to be blamed for failing to take action for events which, due to ineffective pastoral work, they may know nothing about!

Epilogue

Because of the inevitable constraints of space, I have not been able to include previously unpublished examples of essays written by bad and good attenders ('Why I Miss School' or 'Why I Attend School'). However, a few extracts are now presented in the hope that parents, teachers, education welfare officers, educational psychologists, magistrates, social workers, administrators, policy-makers and a host of other interested parties will rethink their own contribution to the process of preventing and treating absenteeism from school. In this technological age, it is vital that all pupils are given the opportunity to develop their skills to their maximum potential. Just as all men are born equal, so all pupils deserve equal treatment in schools, even those pupils who reject the educational opportunities afforded to them. In the long run, this is both the harshest and kindest, as well as the most honest, approach open to professionals.

Comments made by Good Attenders

The following extracts are taken from the good attenders' essays. The Control Group 1 pupils came from the same form as the Persistent Absentees. The Control Group 2 pupils were the academic controls (see Introduction, page 2).

'I love school. Every day is so full of surprises. I really enjoy my lessons but most of all I like being with my friends . . .' (fifth year girl from Control Group 2).

'. . . the best thing about school is taking part in all the various activities which go on during the day. Last week, I played football for the school team, went training to the swimming baths, went on a school trip and started a really exciting project in science . . .' (fourth year boy from Control Group 2).

'The teachers at this school are fabulous, they really help you' (fourth year girl from Control Group 2).

'. . . I don't come to school because I like it. I really come because it's a way of life . . .' (fourth year girl from Control Group 1).

'The best thing about attending school is that you see your mates every day. Sometimes I quite like the lessons. It's funny really, I never thought about why I come to school before. I guess I just do because there's nothing else to do. Really, it's not all that great is it?' (fourth year boy from Control Group 1).

'. . . Last year I used to dream I was in another school. Life is like that. You're never satisfied with what you've got' (fifth year girl from Control Group 1).

'. . . You might think me queer but I quite like coming to school. None of my friends do – or at least they wouldn't admit it. I think I would like it more if the teachers were more interested in you and you got better work to do. That's the problem – the lessons are boring most of the time' (fifth year boy from Control Group 1).

'. . . I don't really know why I keep coming here. One day I think I'll stop' (third year boy from Control Group 1).

Comments made by Persistent Absentees

'. . . I've nothing against the school really. It's just the system' (fifth year male Absentee).

'I miss school because I see no point in going to it. What's the use? Every lesson there's a riot. Tom usually starts it by arguing with the teachers. The girls are bitchy about the boys. I just got fed up' (fourth year male Absentee).

'I suppose I really miss school because I prefer to be at home helping my mother or watching TV than sitting in class learning about nothing important' (fifth year female Absentee).

'. . . if you came from my home you'd understand. My dad's out of work. My gran is ill. My brothers don't help with anything and my mother cries because she's so busy and can't afford to buy us good food or clothes . . .' (fourth year female Absentee).

'. . . I said I'd start to attend better this year. But when I tried, I kept getting in trouble all the time. In the end, I thought it was better to keep out of trouble by staying home. That way you get more peace . . .' (fourth year male Absentee).

'The truth is I never meant to start mising school in the first place. . . . It was a kind of accident because I went to help my cousin. Then it became a kind of habit. . . . I haven't anything against school . . . it's just that I can't catch up with the work any more' (third year female Absentee).

'As you can see, I can't rite, or spelle, or do annythinke – so wats the poient? [*sic*]' (third year male Absentee).

'I hate coming to school and everything about it. It's a dump, a lousy place. I hate the teachers. I hate the work and I hate every day I come because all we do is the same boring stuff. I can't wait to leave next term' (fifth year male Absentee).

These few brief extracts are sufficient to show the diversity of opinion which is so evident in work with bright and less able pupils, good and bad attenders. Surely, there is something fundamentally wrong with our secondary system when schooling for certain sections of the population is so much less rewarding than for others?

If fewer pupils were unhappy about their daily school routines, perhaps there would be less absenteeism, alienation, disaffection and disruption. One of the greatest challenges facing educationists today is to make schools rewarding institutions for *everybody* concerned in the enterprise (Hargreaves, 1982). If this nettle could be grasped, everyone would benefit – able and less able pupils, teachers, parents – indeed, society as a whole.

Appendix 1
Legal Cases Cited in Text

Crump v. Gilmore (1970) 68, LGR, 56
Happe v. Lay (1978) 76, LGR, 313
Hares v. Curtin (1913) 2 KB, 328
Jenkins v. Howell (1949) 2 KB, 218, LCT 168
Neave v. Hills (1919) 121, LT, 225
S (A Minor) (Care order: Education) (1977) 75 Local Government Reports
    787
Shaxted v. Ward (1954) 1 ALL ER 336, LCT 193
Spiers v. Warrington Corporation (1954) 1 QB 61, LCT 165
Surrey County Council v. Ministry of Education (1953) 51 Local Govern-
    ment Reports 319

Appendix 2
Recommended Further Reading

BARRELL, G. R. (1978) *Teachers and the Law* (5th edn). London: Methuen.
BIRD, C., CHESSUM, R., FURLONG, J. and JOHNSON, D. (eds) (1980) *Disaffected
    Pupils*. Brunel: Brunel University Educational Studies Unit.
FRUDE, N. and GAULT, H. (eds) (1984) *Disruptive Behaviour in Schools*. Chichester:
    John Wiley.
GALLOWAY, D., BALL, T., BLOMFIELD, D. and SEYD, R. (1982) *Schools and Disruptive
    Pupils*. Harlow: Longman.

GRUNSELL, R. (1980) *Absent from School: the story of a Truancy Centre*. London: Writers and Readers.

HARGREAVES, D. H. (1982) *Challenge for the Comprehensive School*. London: Routledge and Kegan Paul.

HARGREAVES, D. H., HESTER, S. K. and MELLOR, F. J. (1975) *Deviance in Classrooms*. London: Routledge and Kegan Paul.

HERSOV, L. and BERG, I. (eds) (1980) *Out of School: modern perspectives in truancy and school refusal*. Chichester: John Wiley. (See especially Chapters 1–9 and Chapter 17.)

REID, K. (1981) 'Alienation and persistent school absenteeism', in *Research in Education*, **26**, 31–40.

REID, K. (1982a) 'The self-concept and persistent school absenteeism', in *British Journal of Educational Psychology*, **52**, 2, 179–87.

REID, K. (1982d) 'School organisation and persistent school absenteeism: an introduction to a complex problem', in *School Organisation*, **2**, 1, 45–54.

REID, K. (1983a) 'Institutional factors and persistent school absenteeism', in *Educational Management and Administration*, **11**, 17–27.

REID, K. (1983b) 'Retrospection and persistent school absenteeism', in *Educational Research*, **25**, 2, 110–15.

REID, K. (1983c) 'Differences between the perception of persistent absentees towards parents and teachers', in *Educational Studies*, **9**, 3, 211–19.

REID, K. (1984a) 'Some social, psychological and educational aspects related to persistent school absenteeism', in *Research in Education*, **31**, 63–82.

REID, K. (1984b) 'The behaviour of persistent school absentees', in *British Journal of Educational Psychology*, **54**, 320–30.

REID, K. (1984) 'Disruptive persistent school absentees', in FRUDE, N. and GAULT, H. (eds) *Disruptive Behaviour in Schools*. Chichester: John Wiley.

REYNOLDS, D., JONES, D., ST LEGER, S. and MURGATROYD, S. (1980) 'School factors and truancy' in HERSOV, L. and BERG, I. (eds) *Out of School: modern perspectives in truancy and school refusal*. Chichester: John Wiley.

RUTTER, M., OUSTON, J., MAUGHAN, B. and MORTIMORE, P. (1979) *Fifteen Thousand Hours*. London: Open Books.

TATTUM, D. (1982) *Disruptive Pupils in Schools and Units*. Chichester: John Wiley.

WEST, D. J. (1982) *Delinquency: its roots, careers and prospects*. London: Heinemann.

References and
Bibliography

ABBOTT, E. and BRECKINRIDGE, S. R. (1970) *Truancy and Non-attendance in the Chicago Schools* (2nd edn). New York: Arno Press.

ANDERSON, R. R. (1980) *From 'List D' to Day School*. Dundee: Dundee College of Education.

ANDRIOLA, J. (1943) 'Success and failure in the treatment of 25 truants at a child guidance clinic', in *American Journal of Orthopsychiatry*, **13**, 691–717.

ANDRIOLA, J. (1946) 'Truancy syndrome', in *American Journal of Orthopsychiatry*, **16**, 174–6.

AULD, M. (1976) Report of the Committee of Inquiry into William Tyndale School. London: ILEA.

BACHMAN, J. B., GREEN, S. and WIRTANEN, I. D. (1971) *Youth in Transition*. Volume III: Dropping Out – Problem or Symptom. Woburn, MA: Ann Arbor/Institute for Social Research.

BAKER, J. (1964) *Children in Chancery*. London: Hutchinson.

BALL, N. (1973) 'Elementary school attendance and voluntary effort before 1870', in *History of Education*, **2**, 1, 19–34.

BARNES, J. A. (1979) Observations on the Report of Irregular School Attendance Survey, March 1979. North Western Regional Society of Education Officers.

BARRELL, G. R. (1978) *Teachers and the Law* (5th edn). London: Methuen.

BAUM, T. (1978) 'Surveys of absenteeism: a question of timing', in *Educational Research*, **20**, 3, 226–30.

BAUER, D. (1980) 'Childhood fears in developmental perspective', in HERSOV, L. and BERG, I. (eds) *Out of School: modern perspectives in truancy and school refusal*. Chichester: John Wiley.

BAYH, B. (1977) 'Challenge for the Third Century: Education in a Safe Environment.' Final Report on the Nature and Prevention of School Violence and Vandalism. Washington, DC: United States Government Printing Office.

BEAUMONT, G. R. (1976) 'A comparison of the effect of behavioural counselling and teacher support on the attendance of truants.' Unpublished thesis for Diploma in School Counselling. Swansea: University College of Swansea.

BELSON, W. A. (1975) *Juvenile Theft: the causal factors*. London: Harper and Row.

BERESFORD, P. and CROFT, S. (1982) *Intermediate Treatment: radical, alternative, palliative or extension of social control?* London: Battersea Community Action.

BERG, I. (1980) 'School refusal in early adolescence', in HERSOV, L. and BERG, I. (eds) *Out of School: modern perspectives in truancy and school refusal*. Chichester: John Wiley.

BERG, I., BUTLER, A., HULLIN, R., SMITH, R. and TYRER, S. (1978a) 'Features of children taken to juvenile court for failure to attend school', in *Psychological Medicine*, 8, 447–53.

BERG, I., CONSTERDINE, M., HULLIN, R., MCGUIRE, R. and TYRER, S. (1978b) 'A randomly controlled trial of two court procedures in truancy', in *British Journal of Criminology*, 18, 232–44.

BERG, I., HULLIN, R., MCGUIRE, R. and TYRER, S. (1977) 'Truancy and the courts: research note', in *Journal of Child Psychology and Psychiatry*, 18, 359–65.

BERGER, A. and MITCHELL, G. (1978) 'Multitude of sin bins', in *The Times Educational Supplement*, 7 July 1978.

BERNBAUM, G., PATRICK, H. and REID, K. (1985) 'Postgraduate initial teacher training in England and Wales: perspectives from the SPITE project', in HOPKINS, D. and REID, K. (eds) *Rethinking Teacher Education*. London: Croom Helm.

BIENSTOCK, H. (1967) 'Realities of the job market for the high school dropout', in SCHREIBER, D. (ed.) *Profile of the School Dropout*. New York: Random House.

BILLINGTON, B. J. (1978) 'Patterns of attendance and truancy: a study of attendance and truancy amongst first year comprehensive school pupils', in *Educational Review*, 30, 3, 221–5.

BILLINGTON, B. J. (1979) 'Truants: some personality characteristics', in *Durham and Newcastle Research Review*, 9, 43, 1–6.

BIRD, C., CHESSUM, R., FURLONG, J. and JOHNSON, D. (eds) (1980) *Disaffected Pupils*. Brunel: Brunel University Educational Studies Unit.

BLACK, SIR H. (1979) Report of the Children and Young Persons Review Group. London: HMSO.

BLYTHMAN, M. (1975) 'Truants suffer more from the "disadvantages of life"', in *Scottish Educational Journal*, 58, 80–4.

BOARD OF EDUCATION (1960) *Study of Employee Absenteeism in Chicago Public Schools*. Chicago, Il: Board of Education.

BOOTH, C. (1896) *Life and Labour*, Volume I. London: Macmillan.

BOWEN, D. (1983) 'Why truants, not parents, should carry the can', in *Education*, 158, 22, 411.

BOWLES, S. and GINTIS, H. (1976) *Schooling in Capitalist America*. London: Routledge and Kegan Paul.

BOXALL, M. (1973) 'Nurture groups', in *Concern*, 13, 9–11.

BOYSON, R. (1974) 'The need for realism', in TURNER, B. (ed.) *Truancy*. London: Ward Lock Educational.

BRACE, J. (1982) 'The educational state of Wales', in *Education for Development*, 7, 2, 63–72.

BROOKOVER, W. B., ERIKSON, E. L. and JOINER, L. M. (1967) *Self-concept of Ability and School Achievement* (mimeograph). East Lansing, MI: Michigan State University.

BROOKS, D. B. (1974) 'Contingency contracts with truants', in *Personnel and Guidance Journal*, 52, 5, 315–20.

BROOKS, E. E., BURI, J., BYRNE, E. A. and HUDSON, M. C. (1962) 'Socio-economic factors, parental attitudes and school attendance', in *Social Work*, 7, 4, 103–8.

BROWN, D. (1983) 'Truants, families and schools: a critique of the literature on truancy', in *Educational Review*, 35, 3, 225–35.

BUIST, M. (1980) 'Truants talking', in *Scottish Educational Review*, 12, 1, 40–51.

BURT, C. (1925) *The Young Delinquent*. London: University of London Press Ltd.

BUTLER, N., GILL, R., POMEROY, D. and FEWTRELL, J. (1977) 'Uncovering a gap in the service', in *Community Care*, 3 August, 14–16.

CAIN, J. (1974) 'A study of counselling on pupils displaying an irregular pattern of school attendance.' Unpublished dissertation for Diploma in School Counselling. Swansea: University College of Swansea.

CARMICHAEL, J. (1975) 'Aspects of truancy', in *The Times Educational Supplement (Scotland)*, **487**, 17 April.

CARROLL, H. C. M. (ed.) (1977a) *Absenteeism in South Wales: studies of pupils, their homes and their secondary schools*. Swansea: University College of Swansea Faculty of Education.

CARROLL, H. C. M. (1977b) 'A cross-sectional and longitudinal study of poor and good attenders in a comprehensive school', in CARROLL, H. C. M. (ed.) *Absenteeism in South Wales: studies of pupils, their homes and their secondary schools*. Swansea: University College of Swansea Faculty of Education.

CHAZAN, M. (1962) 'School phobia', in *British Journal of Educational Psychology*, **32**, 209–17.

CHERRY, N. (1976) 'Persistent job changing – is it a problem?', in *Journal of Occupational Psychology*, **49**, 203–21.

CHILDREN'S DEFENSE FUND (1975) *School Suspensions: are they helping children?* Cambridge, MA: Children's Defense Fund.

CICOUREL, A. V. and KITSUSE, J. I. (1963) *The Educational Decision-makers*. New York: Bobbs-Merrill.

CLEGG, A. and MEGSON, B. (1975) *Children in Distress*. Harmondsworth: Penguin.

CLOWARD, R. A. and OHLIN, R. E. (1961) *Delinquency and Opportunity*. London: Routledge and Kegan Paul.

CLYNE, M. B. (1966) *Absent: school refusal as an expression of disturbed family relationships*. London: Tavistock.

COHEN, A. K. (1955) *Delinquent Boys*. Chicago, IL: The Free Press.

COHEN, L. (1976) *Educational Research in Classrooms and Schools*. London: Harper and Row.

COMMITTEE ON LOCAL AUTHORITY AND ALLIED PERSONAL SOCIAL SERVICES (1968) *The Seebohm Report*. London: HMSO.

COOLIDGE, J. C., BRODIE, R. D. and FEENEY, B. (1964) 'A ten year follow-up study of sixty-six school-phobic children', in *American Journal of Orthopsychiatry*, **34**, 675–84.

COOMBS, J. and COOLEY, W. N. (1968) 'Dropouts: in high school and after school', in *American Education Journal*, **5**, 343–63.

COOPER, M. G. (1966) 'School refusal: an enquiry into the part played by school and home', in *Educational Research*, **8**, 33, 223–9.

COOPERSMITH, S. (1967) *The Antecedents of Self-esteem*. New York: Freeman.

CROFT, I. J. and GRYGIER, T. G. (1956) 'Social relationships of truants and juvenile delinquents', in *Human Relations*, **9**, 439–66.

CURTIS, S. J. (1967) *History of Education in Great Britain*. Cambridge: University Tutorial Press.

DAYTON, N. A. (1928) 'Mental deficiency and other factors that influence school attendance', in *Mental Hygiene*, **12**, 794–800. See also: *American Journal of Psychiatry*, **7**, 809–35.

DAVIE, R. (1972) 'The missing year', in *Education Guardian*, 12 September.

DAVIE, R. (1977) 'The interface between education and the social services', in KAHAN, B. (ed.) *Working together for Children and their Families*. London:

DHSS/Welsh Office, HMSO.

DAVIE, R. (1980) 'Promoting school adjustment', in PRINGLE, M. K. (ed.) *A Fairer Future for Children*. London: Macmillan.

DAVIE, R., BUTLER, N. and GOLDSTEIN, H. (1972) *From Birth to Seven*. Harlow: Longman, in association with the National Children's Bureau.

DEPARTMENT OF EDUCATION AND SCIENCE (1975) Survey of absence from secondary and middle schools in England and Wales on Thursday 17 January 1974. London: HMSO.

DEPARTMENT OF HEALTH AND SOCIAL SECURITY/WELSH OFFICE (1977) *Working together for Children and their Families*. Report in 2 volumes. London: HMSO.

DOCKING, J. W. (1980) *Control and Discipline in Schools: perspectives and approaches*. London: Harper and Row.

DOUGLAS, J. W. B. and ROSS, J. M. (1965) 'The effects of absence on primary school performance', in *British Journal of Educational Psychology*, **35**, 28–40.

DOUGLAS, J. W. B. and ROSS, J. M. (1968) 'Adjustment and educational progress', in *British Journal of Educational Psychology*, **38**, 1, 69ff.

DOUGLAS, J. W. B., ROSS, J. M. and SIMPSON, H. R. (1968) *All Our Future*. London: Peter Davies.

DUNHAM, J. (1977) 'The effects of disruptive behaviour on teachers', in *Educational Review*, **29**, 3, 181–7. See also *Educational Research*, **23**, 3, 205–13.

DUTCHMAN-SMITH, M. (1971) 'Section 40 of the Education Act, 1944', in *British Journal of Criminology*, **1**, 85–7.

EATON, M. J. and HOUGHTON, D. M. (1974) 'The attitudes of persistent teenage absentees and regular attenders towards school and home', in *Irish Journal of Psychology*, **2**, 3, 159–75.

EDUCATIONAL INSTITUTE OF SCOTLAND (1975) 'Truancy and indiscipline', in *The Scottish Educational Journal*, 7 March 1975, 256–8.

EDWARDS, N. (1955) *The Courts and the Public Schools*. Chicago, IL: University of Chicago Press.

EKBLOM, P. (1979) 'Police truancy patrols', in *Crime Prevention and the Police*, Home Office Research Study, 55. London: HMSO.

ELLIOTT, R. (1975) 'Some characteristics of school non-attenders assessed at Lisnevin School', in *Community Home Schools Gazette*, **69**, 8, 400–3.

ESTES, H. R., HAYLETT, C. H. and JOHNSON, A. L. (1956) 'Separation and anxiety' in *American Journal of Psychotherapy*, **10**, 682–95.

FARRINGTON, D. P. (1976) 'The roots of delinquency', in *Justice of the Peace*, **140**, 164–6.

FARRINGTON, D. (1980) 'Truancy, delinquency, the home and the school', in HERSOV, L. and BERG, I. (eds) *Out of School: modern perspectives in truancy and school refusal*. Chichester: John Wiley.

FERRI, E. (1976) *Growing Up in a One-Parent Family*. Windsor: NFER.

FINLAYSON, D. S. and LOUGHRAN, J. L. (1976) 'Pupils' perceptions in high and low delinquency schools', in *Educational Research*, **18**, 2, 138–45.

FOGELMAN, K. (1976) *Britain's Sixteen-year-olds*. London: National Children's Bureau.

FOGELMAN, K. (1978) 'School attendance, attainment and behaviour', in *British Journal of Educational Psychology*, **48**, 2, 148–58.

FOGELMAN, K. and RICHARDSON, K. (1974) 'School attendance: some results from the National Child Development Study', in TURNER, B. (ed.) *Truancy*. London: Ward Lock Educational.

FOGELMAN, K., TIBBENHAM, A. and LAMBERT, L. (1980) 'Absence from school: findings from the National Child Development Study', in HERSOV, L. and BERG, I. (eds) *Out of School: modern perspectives in truancy and school refusal*. Chichester: John Wiley.

FRAZER, R. (1979) 'Operation Shoplift', in *Police Review*, 20 July, 1138.

FRICK, W. B. (1964) 'School phobia: a critical review of the literature', in *Merrill-Palmer Quarterly*, 10, 361–73.

FRUDE, N. and GAULT, H. (eds) (1984) *Disruptive Behaviour in Schools*. Chichester: John Wiley.

GALLOWAY, D. (1976a) 'Size of school, socio-economic hardship, suspension rate and persistent unjustified absence from school', in *British Journal of Educational Psychology*, 46, 1, 40–7.

GALLOWAY, D. (1976b) 'Persistent unjustified absence from school', in *Trends in Education*, 30, 22–7.

GALLOWAY, D. (1980a) 'Problems in the assessment and management of persistent absenteeism from school', in HERSOV, L. and BERG, I. (eds) *Out of School: modern perspectives in truancy and school refusal*. Chichester: John Wiley.

GALLOWAY, D. (1980b) 'Exclusion and suspension from school', in *Trends in Education*, 2, 33–8.

GALLOWAY, D. (1982) 'Persistent absence from school', in *Educational Research*, 24, 3, 188–96.

GALLOWAY, D., BALL, T., BLOMFIELD, D. and SEYD, R. (1982) *Schools and Disruptive Pupils*. Harlow: Longman.

GALLOWAY, D., BALL, T. and SEYD, R. (1981a) 'Administrative and legal procedures available to local education authorities in cases of poor school attendance', in *Durham and Newcastle Research Review*, 9, 46, 201–9.

GALLOWAY, D., BALL, T. and SEYD, R. (1981b) 'School attendance following legal or administrative action for unauthorised absence', in *Educational Review*, 33, 1, 53–6. See also: *British Journal of Social Work*, 11, 4, 445–61 and *Social Work Today*, 12, 33, 15–17.

GATH, D. (1972) 'Child guidance and delinquency in a London borough', in *Psychological Medicine*, 2, 185–91.

GIBSON, R. O. (1964) *Frequency of Absence of School Personnel*. Albany, NY: Educational Research Association of New York State.

GILLHAM, B. (1984) 'School organisation and the control of disruptive incidents', in FRUDE, N. and GAULT, H. (eds) *Disruptive Behaviour in Schools*. Chichester: John Wiley.

GOLD, S. (1967) 'Psychiatric assessment of school truanters', *British Journal of Criminology*, 7, 202–6.

GOOD, T. L. and BROPHY, J. E. (1978) *Looking in Classrooms* (2nd edn). New York: Harper and Row.

GRAY, G., SMITH, A. and RUTTER, M. (1980) 'School attendance and the first year of employment', in HERSOV, L. and BERG, I. (eds) *Out of School: modern perspectives in truancy and school refusal*. Chichester: John Wiley.

GRUNSELL, R. (1978) *Born to be Invisible: the story of a school for truants*. London: Macmillan.

GRUNSELL, R. (1980) *Absent from School: the story of a Truancy Centre*. London: Writers and Readers.

HAMBLIN, D. H. (1977) 'Caring and control: the treatment of absenteeism', in

CARROLL, H. C. M. (ed.) *Absenteeism in South Wales*. Swansea: University College of Swansea Faculty of Education.

HAMBLIN, D. H. (1978) *The Teacher and Pastoral Care*. Oxford: Basil Blackwell.

HAMPE, E., MILLER, L., BARRETT, C. and NOBLE, H. (1973) 'Intelligence and school phobia', in *Journal of School Psychology*, **11**, 66–70.

HARGREAVES, D. H. (1967) *Social Relations in a Secondary School*. London: Routledge and Kegan Paul.

HARGREAVES, D. H. (1982) *Challenge for the Comprehensive School*. London: Routledge and Kegan Paul.

HARGREAVES, D. H., HESTOR, S. and MELLOR, F. (1975) *Deviance in Classrooms*. London: Routledge and Kegan Paul.

HARRIS, F. (1974) 'Rebels with a cause', in TURNER, B. (ed.) *Truancy*. London: Ward Lock Educational.

HARROP, L. A. (1983) *Behaviour Modification in the Classroom*. London: Hodder and Stoughton.

HATHAWAY, S. R., REYNOLDS, P. C. and MONACHESI, E. D. (1969) 'Follow-up of the later careers and lives of 1000 boys who dropped out of high school', in *Journal of Consulting and Clinical Psychology*, **33**, 370–80.

HAY, M. (1945) 'Play therapy in wartime: a case of truanting', in *American Journal of Orthopsychiatry*, **15**, 201–12.

HEALY, W. (1915) *The Individual Delinquent*. London: Heinemann.

HERBERT, M. (1974) *Emotional Problems of Development in Children*. London and New York: Academic Press.

HER MAJESTY'S INSPECTORATE (1977) *Ten Good Schools: A Secondary Enquiry*. London: HMSO.

HER MAJESTY'S INSPECTORATE (1982) *Report on the Inspection of Willows High School*. South Glamorgan: Welsh Office.

HER MAJESTY'S STATIONERY OFFICE (1968) Social Work (Scotland) Act, 1968. London and Edinburgh: HMSO.

HER MAJESTY'S STATIONERY OFFICE (1973) *School Transport*. London: HMSO.

HERSOV, L. (1960a) 'Persistent non-attendance at school', in *Journal of Child Psychology and Psychiatry*, **1**, 130–6.

HERSOV, L. (1960b) 'Refusal to go to school', in *Journal of Child Psychology and Psychiatry*, **1**, 137–45.

HERSOV, L. (1976) 'School refusal', in RUTTER, M. and HERSOV, L. (eds) *Child Psychiatry: Modern Approaches*. Oxford: Blackwell Scientific.

HERSOV, L. (1980) 'Hospital in-patient and day-patient treatment of school refusal', in HERSOV, L. and BERG, I. (eds) *Out of School: modern perspectives in truancy and school refusal*. Chichester: John Wiley.

HERSOV, L. and BERG, I. (eds) (1980) *Out of School: modern perspectives in truancy and school refusal*. Chichester: John Wiley.

HODGES, V. (1968) 'Non-attendance at school', in *Educational Research*, **11**, 1, 58–61.

HOGHUGHI, M. (1978) *Troubled and Troublesome*. London: Burnet Books.

HOME OFFICE RESEARCH UNIT (1976) *Further Studies of Female Offenders*, 33. London: HMSO.

HOPKINS, D. (1982) 'Doing research in your own classroom', in *Phi Delta Kappan*, **64**, 4, 274–5.

HOPKINS, D. and REID, K. (1984) 'Masters' degrees in education', in *Journal of Further and Higher Education*, **8**, 1, 10–11.

HOPKINS, D. and REID, K. (1985) *Rethinking Teacher Education*. London: Croom Helm.

HUMPHRIES, S. (1981) *Hooligans or Rebels? An oral history of working-class childhood and youth 1889–1939*. Oxford: Basil Blackwell.

INNER LONDON EDUCATION AUTHORITY (1976) Attendance at school. Schools Sub-committee Document, ILEA 528. London: ILEA.

INNER LONDON EDUCATION AUTHORITY, (1980a) Non-attendance at school: some research findings. Research and Statistics Branch, Document RS 760/80. London: ILEA.

INNER LONDON EDUCATION AUTHORITY (1980b) Research and Statistics Branch, Attendance Survey, Document RS 753/80. London: ILEA. See also: Document RS 791/81.

INNER LONDON EDUCATION AUTHORITY (1981) Perspectives on attendance. Research and Statistics Branch, Document RS 749/80. London: ILEA.

INSTITUTE FOR THE STUDY AND TREATMENT OF DELINQUENCY (1974) 'Truancy in Glasgow: a report by the Glasgow Working Party', in *British Journal of Criminology*, **14**, 3, 248–55.

JARVIS, F. V. (1966) 'The probation service – the effect of the White Paper', in *British Journal of Criminology*, **6**, 2, 152–8.

JENCKS, C. *et al.* (1972) *Inequality*. New York: Basic Books.

JOHNSON, D., RANSOM, E., PACKWOOD, T., BOWDEN, K. and KOGAN, M. (1980) *Secondary Schools and the Welfare Network*. London: Unwin.

JONES, A. (1980) 'The schools' view of persistent non-attendance', in HERSOV, L. and BERG, I. (eds) *Out of School: modern perspectives in truancy and school refusal*. Chichester: John Wiley.

JONES, D. (1974) 'The truant', in *Concern*, 14. London: National Children's Bureau.

JONES, N. (1974) 'Special adjustment units in comprehensive schools', in *Therapeutic Education*, **2**, 2, 21–62. See also: *Therapeutic Education*, **1**, 2, 23–31.

JONES-DAVIES, C. and CAVE, R. (eds) (1976) *The Disruptive Pupil in the Secondary School*. London: Ward Lock Educational.

KAHAN, B. (ed.) (1977) *Working together for Children and their Families*. London: DHSS/Welsh Office, HMSO.

KAHN, J. H. and NURSTEN, J. P. (1968) *Unwillingly to School* (2nd edn). Oxford: Pergamon.

KAHN, J. H. and NURSTEN, J. P. (1971) 'School refusal: revised concepts of diagnosis and treatment', in *Annual Review of Research of the Child Care Association*, **19**, 79–88.

KAHN, J. H., NURSTEN, J. P. and CARROLL, H. C. M. (1981) *Unwillingly to School: School Phobia or School Refusal – a Psychosocial Problem*. Oxford: Pergamon.

KAVANAGH, A. and CARROLL, H. C. M. (1977) 'Pupil attendance in three comprehensive schools: a study of the pupils and their families', in CARROLL, H. C. M. (ed.) *Absenteeism in South Wales*. Swansea: University College of Swansea Faculty of Education.

KELLY, G. (1955) *The Psychology of Personal Constructs*, Volumes 1 and 2. New York: Norton.

KLINE, L. W. (1898) 'The migratory impulse versus the love of home', in *American Journal of Psychology*, **10**, 1–81. See also: *Pediatric Seminar*, **5**, 381–420.

LABON, D. (1973) 'Helping maladjusted children in primary schools', in *Therapeutic Education*, **1**, 2, 14–22.

LALLI, M. and SAVITZ, L. D. (1976) 'The fear of crime in the school enterprise and its consequences', in *Education and Urban Society*, **8**, 4, 401–17.

LANE, D. A. (1977) 'Aspects of the use of behaviour modification in secondary schools', in *British Association for Behavioural Psychotherapy Bulletin*, **5**, 76–9.

LANE, D. A. and MILLAR, R. (1977) 'Dealing with behavioural problems in school: a new development', in *Community Health*, **8**, 155–8.

LASLETT, R. (1977) 'Disruptive and violent pupils: the facts and the fallacies', in *Educational Review*, **29**, 3, 152–62.

LAW, B. (1973) 'An alternative to truancy', in *British Journal of Guidance and Counselling*, **1**, 1, 91–6.

LAWRENCE, J., STEED, D. and YOUNG, P. (1977) 'Disruptive behaviour in a secondary school', *Educational Studies Monograph*, *1*. London: University of London, Goldsmiths' College.

LAWRENCE, J. et al. (1981) *Dialogue on Disruptive Behaviour: a study of a secondary school*. London: PJP Press.

LEACH, D. (1977) 'Teacher perceptions and "problem" pupils', in *Educational Review*, **29**, 3, 188–203.

LEVENTHAL, T. and SILLS, M. (1964) 'Self-image in school phobia', in *American Journal of Orthopsychiatry*, **34**, 4, 685–95.

LEVITT, E. E. (1963) 'Psychotherapy with children: a further evaluation', in *Behaviour Research and Therapy*, **1**, 45–51.

LEWIS, D. G. and MURGATROYD, S. J. (1976) 'The professionalisation of counselling in education and its legal implications', in *British Journal of Guidance and Counselling*, **4**, 1, 2–15.

LITTLE, A. L. (1977) 'Declining pupil performance and the urban environment', in FIELD, F. (ed.) *Education and the Urban Crisis*. London: Routledge and Kegan Paul.

LOCAL GOVERNMENT TRAINING BOARD (1974) *The Role and Training of Education Welfare Officers*. London: HMSO.

LODGE, B. (1977) 'Call to isolate the classroom thugs', in *The Times Educational Supplement*, 15 April.

LOWENSTEIN, L. F. (1975) *Violent and Disruptive Behaviour in Schools*. London: National Association of Schoolmasters.

LUMMIS, C. (1946) 'The relation of school attendance to employment records, army conduct and performance in tests', *British Journal of Educational Psychology*, **16**, 13–19.

MACLURE, S. (1967) *Educational Documents*. London: Methuen.

MARSH, R., ROSSER, E. and HARRE, R. (1978) *The Rules of Disorder*. London: Routledge and Kegan Paul.

MARTIN, F. M., FOX, S. J. and MURRAY, K. (1981) *Children Out of Court*. Edinburgh: Scottish Academic Press.

MAY, D. (1975) 'Truancy, school absenteeism and delinquency', in *Scottish Educational Studies*, **7**, 2, 97–106.

MAYS, J. B. (1964) *Growing up in the City*. Liverpool: Liverpool University Press.

MEAD, M. (1973) *Growing up in New Guinea*. Harmondsworth: Penguin.

MILLER, L., BARRETT, C., HAMPE, E. and NOBLE, H. (1972) 'Comparison of reciprocal inhibition, psychotherapy and waiting list control for phobic children', in *Journal of Abnormal Psychology*, **79**, 269–79.

MILLER, W. M. (1958) 'Lower class culture as a generating milieu of gang delinquency', in *Journal of Social Issues*, **14**, 5–19.

MITCHELL, S. (1972) 'The absentees', in *Education in the North*, **9**, 22–8.

MITCHELL, S. and SHEPHERD, M. (1967) 'The child who dislikes going to school', in *British Journal of Educational Psychology*, **37**, 1, 32–40.

MITCHELL, S. and SHEPHERD, M. (1980) 'Reluctance to go to school', in HERSOV, L. and BERG, I. (eds) *Out of School: modern perspectives in truancy and school refusal.* Chichester: John Wiley.

MODEL, A. N. and SHEPHERD, E. (1958) 'The child who refuses to go to school', in *Medical Officer*, **100**, 39–41.

MONROE, J. (1973) A study of the relationship between truancy and delinquency with reference to a particular comprehensive school for boys since the coming into force of the main sections of the 1969 Children and Young Persons Act. Thesis written for Diploma in Criminology. London: University of London.

MOORE, G. and JARDINE, E. (1983) *Persistent School Absenteeism in Northern Ireland.* Northern Ireland: Department of Education.

MORGAN, R. R. (1975) 'An exploratory study of three procedures to encourage school attendance', in *Psychology in the Schools*, **12**, 2, 209–15.

MORRIS, P. (1978) 'Teacher with a foot in both camps', *Community Care*, **238**, 20–1.

MULLEN, F. A. (1950) 'Truancy and classroom disorder as symptoms of personality problems', in *Journal of Educational Psychology*, **41**, 97–109.

MURGATROYD, S. J. (1974) 'Ethical issues in secondary school counselling', in *Journal of Moral Education*, **4**, 1, 27–37.

MURGATROYD, S. J. and LEWIS, G. (1976) 'The professionalisation of counselling in education and its legal implications', in *British Journal of Guidance and Counselling*, **4**, 2–15.

MURGATROYD, S. J. (1977) 'Pupil perceptions of counsellors: a case study', in *British Journal of Guidance and Counselling*, **5**, 1, 73–8.

MUSGRAVE, P. W. (1965) *The Sociology of Education.* London: Methuen.

NATIONAL ASSOCIATION FOR THE CARE AND REHABILITATION OF OFFENDERS (NACRO) (1978) *The Hammersmith Teenage Project.* Chichester: Barry Rose.

NATIONAL ASSOCIATION OF CHIEF EDUCATION WELFARE OFFICERS (1975) These we Serve. The Report of a Working Party set up to enquire into the Causes of Absence from School. London: NACEWO.

NATIONAL ASSOCIATION OF SCHOOLMASTERS/UNION OF WOMEN TEACHERS (1981) *Discipline or Disorder in Schools: a disturbing choice.* London: NAS/UWT.

NATIONAL EDUCATION ASSOCIATION (1979) 'Teacher opinion polls, 1978–9', in *The Weekly Educational Review*, 9 August.

NATIONAL INSTITUTE OF EDUCATION (1977) *Violent Schools – Safe Schools.* Washington, DC: United States Department of Health, Education and Welfare.

NATIONAL SCHOOL BOARD ASSOCIATION (1979) Report on Discipline in our Big City Schools. Washington, DC: National School Board Association.

NEWSOM REPORT (1963) *Half our Future.* A Report of the Central Advisory Council on Education (England). London: Ministry of Education, HMSO.

O'HAGAN, F. (1977) 'Attitudes of offenders and non-offenders towards school', in *Educational Research*, **19**, 142–6.

PACKWOOD, T. (1976) 'Social workers in schools', *Health and Social Service Journal*, 3 July, 1210–11.

PARTINGTON, J. (1984) *Law and the New Teacher.* London: Holt Saunders.

PATRICK, H., BERNBAUM, G. and REID, K. (1982) 'The Structure and Process of

Initial Teacher Education within Universities in England and Wales.' Leicester: University of Leicester School of Education.

PATRICK, J. (1972) 'The changing pulse of rural life', in *Education in the North*, 9, 15–21.

PITTS, R. and SIMON, A. (1954) 'A psychological and educational study of a group of male prisoners', in *British Journal of Educational Psychology*, 25, 106–21.

POWER, M. J. (1967) 'Delinquent schools?', in *New Society*, 10, 264, 542–3.

POWER, M. J., BENN, R. T. and MORRIS, J. N. (1972) 'Neighbourhood school and juveniles before the courts', in *British Journal of Criminology*, 12, 2, 111–32.

PRING, R. (1978) 'Teacher as researcher', in LAWTON, D., GORDON, P., ING, M., GIBBY, B., PRING, R. and MOORE, T. (eds) *Theory and Practice of Curriculum Studies*. London: Routledge and Kegan Paul.

PRITCHARD, M. and GRAHAM, P. (1966) 'An investigation of a group of patients who have attended both the child and adult departments of the same psychiatric hospital', in *British Journal of Psychiatry*, 112, 603–12.

PUGH, G. (1976) 'Truancy – an abstract of research findings', in *Highlight*, 23. London: National Children's Bureau. See also: *Truancy Centres and Free Schools*. London: National Children's Bureau.

RAFILIDES, M. and HOY, W. K. (1971) 'Student sense of alienation and pupil control orientation of high schools', in *The High School Journal*, 55, 101–11.

RALPHS REPORT (1973) *The Role and Training of Education Welfare Officers*. London: DES.

RALPHSON, H. (1973) 'School absenteeism in a remedial department', in *Remedial Education*, 8, 29–32.

RAVEN, J. (1975) 'School rejection and its amelioration', in *Research Intelligence*, 1, 22–4.

REID, K. (1981) 'Alienation and persistent school absenteeism', in *Research in Education*, 26, 31–40.

REID, K. (1982a) 'The self-concept and persistent school absenteeism', in *British Journal of Educational Psychology*, 52, 2, 179–87.

REID, K. (1982b) 'Case studies and persistent school absenteeism', in *The Counsellor*, 3, 5, 23–30.

REID, K. (1982c) 'Absent, sir', in *Social Work Today*, 13, 42, 12–13.

REID, K. (1982d) 'School organisation and persistent school absenteeism: an introduction to a complex problem', in *School Organisation*, 2, 1, 45–52.

REID, K. (1982e) 'Persistent school absenteeism', in *Westminster Studies in Education*, 5, 27–35.

REID, K. (1983a) 'Institutional factors and persistent school absenteeism', in *Educational Management and Administration*, 11, 17–27.

REID, K. (1983b) 'Retrospection and persistent school absenteeism', in *Educational Research*, 25, 2, 110–15.

REID, K. (1983c) 'Differences between the perception of persistent absentees towards parents and teachers', in *Educational Studies*, 9, 3, 211–19.

REID, K. (1984a) 'Some social, psychological and educational aspects related to persistent school absenteeism', in *Research in Education*, 31, 63–82.

REID, K. (1984b) 'The behaviour of persistent school absentees', in *British Journal of Educational Psychology*, 54, 320–30.

REID, K. (1984c) 'Disruptive persistent school absentees', in FRUDE, N. and GAULT, H. (eds) *Disruptive Behaviour in Schools*. Chichester: John Wiley.

REID, K., BERNBAUM, G. and PATRICK, H. (1980) 'OU Course: Students and PGCE.' Unpublished paper given at UCET Conference, Oxford, November.

REID, K. and JONES, K. (1983) 'Poor relation that's ripe for research', in *The Times Educational Supplement*, 25 March, 4.

REID, K. and KENDALL, L. (1982) 'A review of some recent research into persistent school absenteeism', in *British Journal of Educational Studies*, **XXX**, 3, 295–314.

REYNOLDS, D. (1975) 'When teachers and pupils refuse a truce: the secondary school and the creation of delinquency', in MUNGHAM, G. and PEARSON, G. (eds) *Working Class Youth Culture*. London: Routledge and Kegan Paul.

REYNOLDS, D. (1976) 'The delinquent school', in HAMMERSLEY, M. and WOODS, P. (eds) *The Process of Schooling: a sociological reader*. London: Routledge and Kegan Paul.

REYNOLDS, D. (1977) 'Toward a socio-psychological view of truancy', in KAHAN, B. (ed.) *Working together for Children and their Families*. London: DHSS/Welsh Office, HMSO.

REYNOLDS, D. (1982) 'A state of ignorance', in *Education for Development*, 7, 2, 4–35.

REYNOLDS, D. and MURGATROYD, S. J. (1974) 'Being absent from school', in *British Journal of Law and Society*, **1**, 1, 78–81.

REYNOLDS, D. and MURGATROYD, S. (1977) 'The sociology of schooling and the absent pupil: the school as a factor in the generation of truancy', in CARROLL, H. C. M. (ed.) *Absenteeism in South Wales: studies of pupils, their homes and their secondary schools*. Swansea: University College of Swansea Faculty of Education.

REYNOLDS, D., JONES, D. and ST LEGER, S. (1976) 'Schools do make a difference', in *New Society*, 37, 721, 223–5.

REYNOLDS, D. and JONES, D. (1978) 'Education and the prevention of juvenile delinquency', in TUTT, N. (ed.) *Alternative Strategies for Coping with Crime*. Oxford: Basil Blackwell.

REYNOLDS, D., JONES, D., ST LEGER, S. and MURGATROYD, S. (1980) 'School factors and truancy', in HERSOV, L. and BERG, I. (eds) *Out of School: modern perspectives in truancy and school refusal*. Chichester: John Wiley.

REYNOLDS, D. and REID, K. (1985) 'The second stage – towards a reconceptualisation of theory and methodology in school effectiveness studies', in REYNOLDS, D. (ed.) for the School Differences Research Group. *Studying School Effectiveness*. Lewes: Falmer Press.

REYNOLDS, D. and SULLIVAN, M. (1979) 'Bringing schools back in', in BARTON, L. A. (ed.) *Schools, Pupils and Deviance*. London: Nafferton.

ROBERTS, A. (1972) 'Attendance: How the battle was won', in *Education in the North*, 9, 10–14.

ROBINS, L. N. (1966) *Deviant Children Grown Up*. A Sociological and Psychiatric Study of Sociopathic Personality. Baltimore, OH: Williams and Wilkins.

ROBINS, L. N., RATCLIFF, K. S. and WEST, P. A. (1979) 'School achievement in two generations: a study of 88 urban black families', in SHAMSIE, S. J. (ed.) *New Directions in Children's Mental Health*. New York: Spectrum.

ROBINS, L. N. and RATCLIFF, K. S. (1980) 'The long-term outcome of truancy', in HERSOV, L. and BERG, I. (ed.) *Out of School: modern perspectives in truancy and school refusal*. Chichester: John Wiley.

ROBINSON, M. (1978) *Schools and Social Work*. London: Routledge and Kegan Paul.

ROSE, G. and MARSHALL, T. F. (1974) *Counselling and School Social Work*. Chichester: John Wiley.

ROWAN, P. (1976) 'Short-term sanctuary', in *The Times Educational Supplement*, 2 April, 21–4.

ROXBURGH, J. M. (1971) *The School Board of Glasgow, 1873–1919*. London: ULP Ltd for Scottish Council for Research in Education. Publication 63.

ROY, W. (1983) *Teaching under Attack*. London: Croom Helm.

RUBEL, R. J. (1977) *The Unruly School*. Lexington, MA: Lexington.

RUBINSTEIN, D. (1969) *School Attendance in London, 1870–1904*. Hull: Hull University Press.

RUTTER, M. (1967) 'A children's behaviour questionnaire for completion by teacher: preliminary findings', in *Journal of Child Psychology and Psychiatry*, **8**, 1–11.

RUTTER, M. (1972) *Maternal Deprivation Reassessed*. Harmondsworth: Penguin.

RUTTER, M. (1973) 'Why are London children so disturbed?', in *Proceedings of the Royal Society of Medicine*, **66**, 1221–5.

RUTTER, M. and MADGE, N. (1976) *Cycles of Disadvantage*. London: Heinemann.

RUTTER, M., OUSTON, J., MAUGHAN, B. and MORTIMORE, P. (1979) *Fifteen Thousand Hours*. London: Open Books.

RUTTER, M., TIZARD, J. and WHITMORE, K. (1970) *Education, Health and Behaviour*. London: Longman.

RUTTER, M. and YULE, W. (1976) 'Reading difficulties', in RUTTER, M. and HERSOV, L. (eds) *Child Psychiatry: modern approaches*. Oxford: Blackwell Scientific

SASSI, L. C. F. (1973) 'The effect of counselling on school truants.' Unpublished dissertation for Diploma in School Counselling. Swansea: University College of Swansea.

SCOTTISH ASSOCIATION FOR THE STUDY OF DELINQUENCY (SASD) (1977) *'Fa Wid be a Scholar': a study in truancy*. Edinburgh: SASD.

SCOTTISH EDUCATION DEPARTMENT (1977) Truancy and Indiscipline in Schools in Scotland (The Pack Report). London: HMSO.

SEABROOK, J. (1974) 'Talking to truants', in TURNER, B. (ed.) *Truancy*. London: Ward Lock Educational.

SHELTON, J. (1976) 'Application of labelling analysis to the study of non-attendance', in *Journal of the International Association of Pupil Personnel Workers*, **20**, 3, 149–51.

SHEPHERD, M., OPPENHEIM, B. and MITCHELL, S. (1971) *Childhood Behaviour and Mental Health*. London: University of London Press Ltd.

SHIPMAN, M. (1968) *Sociology of the School*. London: Longman.

SHOSTAK, J. (1982) 'Black side of school', in *The Times Educational Supplement*, 25 June, 23.

SIMPSON, I. J. (1947) *Education in Aberdeenshire before 1872*. London: University of London Press Ltd for the Scottish Council for Research in Education. Pubn 25.

SKINNER, A., PLATTS, H. and HILL, B. (1983) *Disaffection from School: issues and interagency responses*. Leicester: National Youth Bureau.

SMITHELLS, R. (1977) 'Confidentiality', in KAHAN, B. (ed.) *Working together for*

Children and their Families. London: DHSS/Welsh Office, HMSO.

STENHOUSE, L. (1975) *An Introduction to Curriculum Research and Development*. London: Heinemann.

STINCHCOMBE, A. L. (1964) *Rebellion in a High School*. Chicago, IL: Quadrangle.

ST-JOHN BROOKS, C. (1982) 'Young people in a strange new world – loose in the city: the underworld of roaming children', in *New Society*, **61**, 1036, 491–4.

STOTT, D. H. (1966) *Studies of Troublesome Children*. London: Tavistock.

STOTT, D. H. and WILSON, D. M. (1968) 'The prediction of early-adult criminality from school-age behaviour', in *International Journal of Social Psychiatry*, **14**, 5–8.

STONE, J. and TAYLOR, F. (1975) 'Is your child fit for school?' in *Where*, **102**, 63–6.

STRATHCLYDE REGIONAL COUNCIL (SRC) (1977) Report on School Attendance. Glasgow: Strathclyde Regional Council Department of Education.

STUBBS, M. and DELAMONT, S. (1976) *Explorations in Classroom Observation*. Chichester: John Wiley.

SULLIVAN, R. and RICHES, S. (1976) 'On your marks: interviews with truants in East London', in *Youth Social Work Bulletin*, **3**, 5, 8–10.

SWANSTROM, T. E. (1967) 'Out-of-school youth', in SCHREIBER, D. (ed.) *Profile of the School Dropout*. New York: Random House.

TATTUM, D. (1982) *Disruptive Pupils in Schools and Units*. Chichester: John Wiley.

TAYLOR, G. and SAUNDERS, J. B. (1976) *The Law of Education* (8th edn). London: Butterworth.

TEICHER, J. D. (1973) 'A solution to the chronic problems of living: adolescent attempted suicide', in SCHOOLAR, J. C. (ed.) *Current Issues in Adolescent Psychiatry*. New York: Brunner/Mazel.

TENNENT, T. G. (1970) 'Truancy and stealing: a comparative study of Education Act cases and property offenders', in *British Journal of Psychiatry*, **116**, 535, 587–92. See also: *British Journal of Criminology*, **10**, 2, 175–80.

TENNENT, T. G. (1971) 'School non-attendance and delinquency', in *Educational Research*, **13**, 3, 185–90.

TERRY, F. (1975) 'Absence from school', in *Youth in Society*, **11**, 7–10.

THOMAS, J. (1982) *Case Proceedings for School Non-attendance and their Outcomes* (Information Sheet). Leicester: National Youth Bureau.

TIBBENHAM, A. (1977) 'Housing and truancy', in *New Society*, **39**, 753, 501–2.

TRIGG, J. E. (1973) 'Focus on the absent minority', in *Special Education*, **62**, 2, 24–8.

TUMELTY, A. (1976) 'A study of the effectiveness of peer counselling of school truants.' Unpublished dissertation for Diploma in School Counselling. Swansea: University College of Swansea.

TURNER, B. (1974) *Truancy*. London: Ward Lock Educational.

TYERMAN, M. J. (1958) 'A research into truancy', in *British Journal of Educational Psychology*, **28**, 3, 217–25. See also: Unpublished PhD thesis on Truancy. London: University of London.

TYERMAN, M. J. (1965) 'Absence from school and its treatment', in *Slow Learning Child*, **12**, 2, 113–18.

— TYERMAN, M. J. (1968) *Truancy*. London: University of London Press Ltd.

TYERMAN, M. J. (1971) 'Truancy and school phobia', in *Bulletin of the British Psychological Society*, **24**, 83, 155–6.

TYERMAN, M. J. (1972) 'Absent from school', in *Trends in Education*, **26**, 14–20.

TYRER, P. and TYRER, S. (1974) 'School refusal, truancy and adult neurotic illness', in *Psychological Medicine*, **4**, 416–21.

UNDEB CENEDLAETHOL ATHRAWON CYMRU (1975) A Report by a Sub-committee of members of UCAC on Truancy and Disruptive Behaviour in Schools. Cardiff: UCAC.

UNITED STATES OFFICE OF EDUCATION (1960) State Legislation on School Attendance, *Circular, 615*. Washington, DC: USOE.

VARLAAM, A. (1974) 'Educational attainment and behaviour at school', in *Greater London Intelligence Quarterly*, **29**, 29–37.

VAUGHAN, M. (1976) 'Welsh tradition blamed for the high rate of truancy', in *The Times Educational Supplement*, **3174**, 10.

WATKIN, A. (1975) 'Truancy in Wales: facts and figures', in *Education*, **75**, 423–4.

WEDGE, P. and PROSSER, H. (1973) *Born to Fail*. London: Arrow in association with the National Children's Bureau.

WEINER, G. and HARPER, P. A. (1966) 'Low birth weight – a high risk factor', in *Journal of the American Medical Association*, **195**, 35–6.

WEST, D. J. and FARRINGTON, D. P. (1973) *Who Becomes Delinquent?* London: Heinemann.

WEST, D. J. and FARRINGTON, D. P. (1977) *The Delinquent Way of Life*. London: Heinemann.

WEST, D. J. (1982) *Delinquency: its roots, careers and prospects*. London: Heinemann.

WEST, E. G. (1965) *Education and the State*. London: Institute of Economic Affairs.

WEST GLAMORGAN (1980) Research into Non-attendance at School: Final Report – Stage III. Swansea: West Glamorgan County Education Committee.

WHITE, D. J. and PEDDIE, M. (1978) 'Patterns of absenteeism in primary and secondary schools', in *Scottish Educational Review*, **10**, 2, 37–44.

WHITE, L. F. W. (1970) 'Parents and the Law. Children before the Courts.' *Where*, **49**, 78–9.

WILKIN, D. (1979) *Caring for the Mentally Handicapped Child*. London: Croom Helm.

WILLIAMS, P. (1974) 'Collecting the figures', in TURNER, B. (ed.) *Truancy*. London: Ward Lock Educational.

WILLIS, P. E. (1977) *Learning to Labour: how working-class kids get working-class jobs*. Aldershot: Saxton House.

WITHRINGTON, D. (1975) 'Anxieties over withdrawal from school: historical comment', in *Research Intelligence*, **1**, 20–2.

WOLSTENHOLME, F. and KOLVIN, I. (1980) 'Social workers in schools: the teachers' response', in *British Journal of Guidance and Counselling*, **8**, 1, 44–56.

YORK, R., HERON, J. and WOLFF, S. (1972) 'Exclusion from school', in *Journal of Child Psychology and Psychiatry*, **13**, 259–66.

YULE, W. (1977) 'Behaviour approaches', in RUTTER, M. and HERSOV, L. (eds) *Child Psychiatry: modern approaches*. Oxford: Blackwell Scientific.

YULE, W., HERSOV, L. and TRESEDER, J. (1980) 'Behavioural treatments of school refusal', in HERSOV, L. and BERG, I. (eds) *Out of School: modern perspectives in truancy and school refusal*. Chichester: John Wiley.

Index

acceptable excuses, 26–7
adjustment characteristics, 62
Administrative Memorandum No.
    531, 28
age differences, 14–17
anxiety and non-attendance, 72

behaviour, 64–5
Bicester scheme, 121–2
Black Committee, 24
Bristol Social Adjustment Guides, 69
Brookover Self-concept of
    Academic Ability Scale, 73
bullying, 89–90

career aspirations, 126–7
case data, 96–106, 112, 135–7
case studies, 3–5, 28, 44–7, 48,
    53–4, 65–7, 74–9, 89, 128–9,
    132–4
categories of persistent absence,
    48–51
Children's and Young Persons'
    Act, 1969, 23, 25, 29–31, 35, 36,
    39
combatting non-attendance, 100–1
compulsory school age, 26
Coopersmith Self-esteem
    Inventory, 73, 74
counselling, 1, 109–10
Court procedures, 31–4
Criminal Law Act, 1977, 26
criticisms of court decisions, 37–9
criticisms of teachers, 99
curriculum and absenteeism, 87–8
curriculum and examinations, 88–9

definitions, 6–7
delinquency, 64
dislike of school, 86
disruptive behaviour, 65–6

Education Act, 1870, 12, 13
Education Act, 1918, 12, 13
Education Act, 1944, 7, 23, 25, 26,
    29–31, 36, 37
Education Act, 1962, 26
Education Act, 1981, 23, 26
Education School Leaving Dates
    Act, 1976, 26
Education (Scotland) Act, 1962, 24
Education Welfare Service, 24, 40,
    120–1
educational facets *per se*, 85–95
Employment of Children Act,
    1973, 128

form registers, 28–9

generic absentees, 50
good practice, 119–23
good teaching, 103
guidance of truants, 108–18
guidance within schools, 113

help with problems, 102
Her Majesty's Inspectorate (HMI),
    17, 29, 80, 83
historical aspects, 11–13
Home Office, 38
home problems, 52–6, 104–5

incidence of truancy, 13–14
in loco parentis concept, 40
illegal employment, 128
inside schools, 96–107
institutional absentees, 49
institutional aspects, 80–5
intelligence, 61–2

labelling, 58–9
law, 23–40

leadership, 119
Leeds, 28
legal cases, 26, 27, 29, 138
life-styles of absentees, 74–7
Local Authority Social Services
  Act, 1970, 31

Manpower Services Commission,
  20
medical reasons, 41–3

non-attendance at school and work,
  127–8
Northern Ireland, 19, 44

Pack Committee Report, 6, 14, 38,
  52, 53
parental attitudes, 48, 106
parental responsibilities, 25–6
peer-group relationships, 90–1
personal characteristics, 59–61
personality and truancy, 71–4
PGCE courses, 18
philosophy of schools, 120
practical implications, 21–2,
  39–49, 50–1, 55–6, 67, 77–9,
  84, 93–5, 106–7, 116–18, 122–3,
  129–30
prosecution statistics, 36–7
prospective outlook, 131–5
psychological absence, 70
psychological absentees, 49
psychological aspects, 68–79
psychological theories, 68–70
pupil fantasy, 129
pupil workloads, 103
pupils' perceptions, 85–6, 98–106
Pupils Registration Regulations,
  1956, 29

race, 39
Ralphs Report, 36
reasons for missing school, 41–51
relationships with teachers, 92–3
Repertory Grid technique, 71,
  74–7
role of the school, 27–8; *see also*
  appropriate sections of most
  chapters

School Attendance Orders, 26, 35,
  36, 43, 44
school change, 99–100
school differences, 82–3, 85
school likes and dislikes, 98–9
school rules and punishment, 91–2
school transfers, 86
Schools Regulations, 1959, 27
Scotland, 23–4, 37
self-concept, 72–4
self-concept therapy, 78
sex differences, 14–17
Sheffield, 28, 29, 33, 35–6, 38,
  43–4
single or group absenteeism, 47–8
social anthropological approach,
  96–8
social and psychological aspects,
  57–67
social aspects, 52–6; *see also*
  appropriate sections of most
  chapters
social work and truancy, 110–13
Social Work (Scotland) Act, 1968,
  24
South Wales, 17–19, 44–6, 94, 96
special units and free schools,
  114–16
staff attitudes, 113–14
Strathclyde Regional Council, 24,
  53

teacher-as-researcher concept, 84
teaching malaise, 57
Technical and Vocational
  Educational Initiative (TVEI),
  20, 130
theory, 8–10
traditional or typical absentees,
  48–9
truancy and adult life, 124–30
truants' feelings, 46–7

United States of America, 13,
  19–20, 39, 94

Wales, 17–19, 27; *see also* South
  Wales
West Glamorgan, 18